Microsoft

MOS 2013 Study Guide for Microsoft Excel Expert

Mark Dodge

PUBLISHED BY
Microsoft Press
A Division of Microsoft Corporation
One Microsoft Way
Redmond, Washington 98052-6399

Library of Congress Control Number: 2013941818
ISBN: 978-0-7356-6921-5

Printed and bound in the United States of America.

6   16

Microsoft Press books are available through booksellers and distributors worldwide. If you need support related to this book, email Microsoft Press Book Support at mspinput@microsoft.com. Please tell us what you think of this book at http://www.microsoft.com/learning/booksurvey.

Microsoft and the trademarks listed at http://www.microsoft.com/en-us/legal/intellectualproperty/trademarks/en-us.aspx are trademarks of the Microsoft group of companies. All other marks are property of their respective owners.

The example companies, organizations, products, domain names, email addresses, logos, people, places, and events depicted herein are fictitious. No association with any real company, organization, product, domain name, email address, logo, person, place, or event is intended or should be inferred.

This book expresses the author's views and opinions. The information contained in this book is provided without any express, statutory, or implied warranties. Neither the authors, Microsoft Corporation, nor its resellers, or distributors will be held liable for any damages caused or alleged to be caused either directly or indirectly by this book.

Acquisitions Editor: Rosemary Caperton
Editorial Production: Online Training Solutions, Inc. (OTSI)
Technical Reviewer: Rob Carr (OTSI)
Copyeditor: Jaime Odell (OTSI)
Indexer: Krista Wall (OTSI)
Cover: Microsoft Press Brand Team

Contents

Introduction vii

   Who this book is for vii

   How this book is organized viii

   Download the practice files viii

      Sidebar: Adapting exercise steps x

   Ebook edition xi

   Get support and give feedback xi

      Errata xi

      We want to hear from you xii

      Stay in touch xii

Taking a Microsoft Office Specialist exam xiii

   Microsoft Office Specialist certification xiii

   Selecting a certification path xiii

   Test-taking tips xiv

   Certification benefits xvi

   For more information xvi

Exams 77-427 and 77-428 Microsoft Excel 2013 Expert

   Prerequisites 1

1   Manage and share workbooks   3

   1.1 Manage multiple workbooks 3

      Modifying workbook templates 4

      Managing workbook versions 6

      Copying styles between templates 7

      Sidebar: Merging styles that have the same name 8

      Copying macros between workbooks 9

What do you think of this book? We want to hear from you!

Microsoft is interested in hearing your feedback so we can continually improve our books and learning resources for
you. To participate in a brief online survey, please visit:

microsoft.com/learning/booksurvey

Connecting to external data 10

Sidebar: About the Excel Data Model. 11

Sidebar: Editing formula links 12

Practice tasks 15

1.2 Prepare workbooks for review. 16

Tracking changes. 16

Sidebar: Setting tracking options 16

Protecting workbooks for sharing 19

Sidebar: Properties vs. metadata. 24

Practice tasks 29

1.3 Manage workbook changes. 30

Displaying all changes. 30

Reviewing changes 31

Managing comments 32

Merging workbooks 33

Identifying errors. 35

Troubleshooting by using tracing. 37

Sidebar: Tracing formulas in separate worksheets 39

Practice tasks 40

Objective review 40

2   Apply custom formats and layouts   41

2.1 Apply custom data formats 41

Creating custom formats (number, time, date). 42

Using advanced Fill Series options 51

Practice tasks 54

2.2 Apply advanced conditional formatting and filtering. 55

Creating custom conditional formats 56

Using functions to format cells 58

Creating advanced filters 60

Sidebar: Managing conditional formatting rules 61

Practice tasks 63

2.3 Apply custom styles and templates 63

Creating custom templates 63

Creating and modifying cell styles 65

Creating custom color and font formats 66

Creating themes. 68

Creating form fields. 70

Sidebar: Controlling the tab order of objects 73

Practice tasks 75

2.4 Prepare workbooks for internationalization and accessibility 76

Modifying worksheets for use with accessibility tools 76

Displaying data in multiple international formats 79

Sidebar: Proofing in other languages. 80

Sidebar: Managing multiple options for body and heading fonts 83

Practice tasks 83

Objective review 84

3   Create advanced formulas   85

3.1 Apply functions in formulas 85

Using nested functions 87

Using the IF, AND, and OR functions 87

Using the SUMIFS, AVERAGEIFS, and COUNTIFS functions 88

Using financial functions 90

Practice tasks 95

3.2 Look up data by using functions 96

Using the VLOOKUP and HLOOKUP functions 96

Using the LOOKUP function 98

Using the TRANSPOSE function 98

Practice tasks 100

3.3 Apply advanced date and time functions 100

Using the NOW and TODAY functions 101

Using functions to serialize dates and times 102

Sidebar: Concatenating text in formulas 103

Practice tasks 105

3.4 Create scenarios 105

Using what-if analysis tools 106

Sidebar: Enabling iterative calculations 107

Sidebar: Using the watch window. 110

Using the Scenario Manager 111

Sidebar: Merging scenarios 112

Consolidating data 113

Practice tasks 117

Objective review 117

4   Create advanced charts and tables   119

4.1 Create advanced chart elements. 119

Adding trendlines to charts 120

Sidebar: Working with other elements. 122

Creating dual-axis charts 123

Creating custom chart templates 127

Practice tasks 129

4.2 Create and manage PivotTables 129

Creating PivotTables 129

Modifying field selections and options 134

Creating slicers. 137

Using PowerPivot. 139

Practice tasks 148

4.3 Create and manage PivotCharts 148

Creating PivotCharts. 149

Sidebar: Viewing chart animations 150

Manipulating options in existing PivotCharts 150

Applying styles to PivotCharts 152

Practice tasks 153

Objective review 153

Index. 155

About the author 167

Survey page. 168

What do you think of this book? We want to hear from you!

Microsoft is interested in hearing your feedback so we can continually improve our books and learning resources for you. To participate in a brief online survey, please visit:

microsoft.com/learning/booksurvey

Introduction

The Microsoft Office Specialist (MOS) certification program has been designed to validate your knowledge of and ability to use programs in the Microsoft Office 2013 suite of programs, Microsoft Office 365, and Microsoft SharePoint. This book has been designed to guide you in studying the types of tasks you are likely to be required to demonstrate in Exam 77-427: Microsoft Excel 2013 Expert Part One, and Exam 77-428: Microsoft Excel 2013 Expert Part Two.

> **See Also** For information about the tasks you are likely to be required to demonstrate in Exam 77-420: Microsoft Excel 2013, see *MOS 2013 Study Guide for Microsoft Excel* by Joan Lambert (Microsoft Press, 2013).

Who this book is for

MOS 2013 Study Guide for Microsoft Excel Expert is designed for experienced Excel users seeking Microsoft Office Specialist Expert certification in Excel 2013. This certification requires that the candidate pass two exams. This book covers the objectives of both exams.

MOS exams for individual programs are practical rather than theoretical. You must demonstrate that you can complete certain tasks or projects rather than simply answering questions about program features. The successful MOS certification candidate will have at least six months of experience using all aspects of the application on a regular basis; for example, using Excel at work or school to manage and share workbooks, apply and share custom formatting, present data in PivotTables and Pivot Charts, create models and scenarios, and create advanced formulas by using functions.

As a certification candidate, you probably have a lot of experience with the program you want to become certified in. Many of the procedures described in this book will be familiar to you; others might not be. Read through each study section and ensure that you are familiar with not only the procedures included in the section, but also the concepts and tools discussed in the review information. In some cases, graphics depict the tools you will use to perform procedures related to the skill set. Study the graphics and ensure that you are familiar with all the options available for each tool.

How this book is organized

The exam coverage is divided into chapters representing broad skill sets that correlate to the functional groups covered by the exams, and each chapter is divided into sections addressing groups of related skills that correlate to the exam objectives. Each section includes review information, generic procedures, and practice tasks you can complete on your own while studying. When necessary, we provide practice files you can use to work through the practice tasks. You can practice the procedures in this book by using the practice files supplied or by using your own files.

Throughout this book, you will find Strategy tips that present information about the scope of study that is necessary to ensure that you achieve mastery of a skill set and are successful in your certification effort.

The exam objectives are divided into four functional groups. The mapping of the exam objectives to the certification exams is shown in the following table.

Functional group	Objectives covered by Exam 77-427	Objectives covered by Exam 77-428
1 Manage and Share Workbooks	1.3 Manage Workbook Changes	1.1 Manage Multiple Workbooks 1.2 Prepare a Workbook Review
2 Apply Custom Formats and Layouts	2.2 Apply Advanced Conditional Formatting and Filtering 2.4 Prepare a Workbook for Internationalization and Accessibility	2.1 Apply Custom Data Formats 2.3 Apply Custom Styles and Templates
3 Create Advanced Formulas	3.2 Look Up Data with Functions 3.3 Apply Advanced Date and Time Functions	3.1 Apply Functions in Formulas 3.4 Create Scenarios
4 Create Advanced Charts and Tables	4.1 Create Advanced Chart Elements 4.2 Create and Manage PivotTables	4.3 Create and Manage Pivot Charts

Candidates must pass both exams to earn the Microsoft Office Specialist Expert certification in Excel 2013.

Download the practice files

Before you can complete the practice tasks in this book, you need to download the book's practice files to your computer. These practice files can be downloaded from the following page: *http://aka.ms/mosExcelExp2013/files*

Important The Excel 2013 program is not available from this website. You should purchase and install that program before using this book.

If you would like to be able to refer to the completed versions of practice files at a later time, you can save the practice files that you modify while working through the exercises in this book. If you save your changes and later want to repeat the exercise, you can download the original practice files again.

The following table lists the practice files for this book.

Folder and functional group	Files
MOSExcel2013Expert\Objective1	*ExcelExpert_1-1a.xltx*
1 Manage and share workbooks	*ExcelExpert_1-1b.accdb*
	ExcelExpert_1-1c.xlsx
	ExcelExpert_1-1d.xlsx
	ExcelExpert_1-2.xlsx
	ExcelExpert_1-3a.xlsx
	ExcelExpert_1-3b.xlsx
	ExcelExpert_1-3c.xlsx
	ExcelExpert_1-3d.xlsx
	ExcelExpert_1-3e.xlsx
MOSExcel2013Expert\Objective2	*ExcelExpert_2-1.xlsx*
2 Apply custom formats and layouts	*ExcelExpert_2-2.xlsx*
	ExcelExpert_2-3.xlsx
	ExcelExpert_2-4.xlsx
MOSExcel2013Expert\Objective3	*ExcelExpert_3-1a.xlsx*
3 Create advanced formulas	*ExcelExpert_3-1b.xlsx*
	ExcelExpert_3-2.xlsx
	ExcelExpert_3-3.xlsx
	ExcelExpert_3-4a.xlsx
	ExcelExpert_3-4b.xlsx
	ExcelExpert_3-4c.xlsx
	ExcelExpert_3-4d.xlsx
MOSExcel2013Expert\Objective4	*ExcelExpert_4-1.xlsx*
4 Create advanced charts and tables	*ExcelExpert_4-2a.xlsx*
	ExcelExpert_4-2b.xlsx
	ExcelExpert_4-3.xlsx

Adapting exercise steps

The screen images shown in this book were captured at a screen resolution of 1024 × 768, at 100 percent magnification. If your settings are different, the ribbon on your screen might not look the same as the one shown in this book. For example, you might have more or fewer buttons in each of the groups, the buttons you have might be represented by larger or smaller icons than those shown, or the group might be represented by a button that you click to display the group's commands. As a result, exercise instructions that involve the ribbon might require a little adaptation. Our instructions use this format:

→ On the **Insert** tab, in the **Illustrations** group, click the **Chart** button.

If the command is in a list or on a menu, our instructions use this format:

→ On the **Home** tab, in the **Editing** group, click the **Find** arrow and then, on the **Find** menu, click **Advanced Find**.

> **Tip** On subsequent instances of instructions located on the same tab or in the same group, the instructions are simplified to reflect that we've already established the working location.

If differences between your display settings and ours cause a button to appear differently on your screen than it does in this book, you can easily adapt the steps to locate the command. First click the specified tab, and then locate the specified group. If a group has been collapsed into a group list or under a group button, click the list or button to display the group's commands. If you can't immediately identify the button you want, point to likely candidates to display their names in ScreenTips.

If you prefer not to have to adapt the steps, set up your screen to match ours while you read and work through the exercises in this book.

In this book, we provide instructions based on the traditional keyboard and mouse input methods. If you're using the program on a touch-enabled device, you might be giving commands by tapping with a stylus or your finger. If so, substitute a tapping action any time we instruct you to click a user interface element. Also note that when we tell you to enter information, you can do so by typing on a keyboard, tapping an on-screen keyboard, or even speaking aloud, depending on your computer setup and your personal preferences.

Ebook edition

If you're reading the ebook edition of this book, you can do the following:

- Search the full text
- Print
- Copy and paste

You can purchase and download the ebook edition from our Microsoft Press site at oreilly.com, which you can find at:

http://aka.ms/mosExcelExp2013

Get support and give feedback

The following sections provide information about getting help with this book and contacting us to provide feedback or report errors.

Errata

We've made every effort to ensure the accuracy of this book and its companion content. Any errors that have been reported since this book was published are listed on our Microsoft Press site:

http://aka.ms/mosExcelExp2013/errata

If you find an error that is not already listed, you can report it to us through the same page.

If you need additional support, send an email message to Microsoft Press Book Support at:

mspinput@microsoft.com

Please note that product support for Microsoft software is not offered through the preceding addresses.

We want to hear from you

At Microsoft Press, your satisfaction is our top priority, and your feedback our most valuable asset. Please tell us what you think of this book at:

http://www.microsoft.com/learning/booksurvey

The survey is short, and we read every one of your comments and ideas. Thanks in advance for your input!

Stay in touch

Let's keep the conversation going! We're on Twitter at:

http://twitter.com/MicrosoftPress

Taking a Microsoft Office Specialist exam

Desktop computing proficiency is increasingly important in today's business world. When screening, hiring, and training employees, employers can feel reassured by relying on the objectivity and consistency of technology certification to ensure the competence of their workforce. As an employee or job seeker, you can use technology certification to prove that you already have the skills you need to succeed, saving current and future employers the time and expense of training you.

Microsoft Office Specialist certification

Microsoft Office Specialist certification is designed to assist employees in validating their skills with Office programs. The following certification paths are available:

- A Microsoft Office Specialist (MOS) is an individual who has demonstrated proficiency by passing a certification exam in one or more Office programs, including Microsoft Word, Excel, PowerPoint, Outlook, Access, OneNote, or SharePoint.

- A Microsoft Office Specialist Expert (MOS Expert) is an individual who has taken his or her knowledge of Office to the next level and has demonstrated by passing the required certification exams that he or she has mastered the more advanced features of Word or Excel.

Selecting a certification path

When deciding which certifications you would like to pursue, you should assess the following:

- The program and program version or versions with which you are familiar
- The length of time you have used the program and how frequently you use it
- Whether you have had formal or informal training in the use of that program
- Whether you use most or all of the available program features
- Whether you are considered a go-to resource by business associates, friends, and family members who have difficulty with the program

Candidates for MOS-level certification are expected to successfully complete a wide range of standard business tasks, such as formatting a document or worksheet and its content; creating and formatting visual content; or working with SharePoint lists, libraries, Web Parts, and dashboards. Successful candidates generally have six or more months of experience with the specific Office program, including either formal, instructor-led training or self-study using MOS-approved books, guides, or interactive computer-based materials.

Candidates for MOS Expert–level certification are expected to successfully complete more complex tasks that involve using the advanced functionality of the program. Successful candidates generally have at least six months, and may have several years, of experience with the programs, including formal, instructor-led training or self-study using MOS-approved materials.

Test-taking tips

Every MOS certification exam is developed from a set of exam skill standards (referred to as the objective domain) that are derived from studies of how the Office programs are used in the workplace. Because these skill standards dictate the scope of each exam, they provide critical information about how to prepare for certification. This book follows the structure of the full objective domain for Excel Expert certification; see "How this book is organized" in the Introduction for more information.

The MOS certification exams are performance based and require you to complete business-related tasks or projects in the program for which you are seeking certification. For example, you might be presented with a file and told to do something specific with it, or presented with a sample document and told to create it by using resources provided for that purpose. Your score on the exam reflects how well you perform the requested tasks or complete the project within the allotted time.

Here is some helpful information about taking the exam:

- Keep track of the time. Your exam time does not officially begin until after you finish reading the instructions provided at the beginning of the exam. During the exam, the amount of time remaining is shown at the bottom of the exam interface. You can't pause the exam after you start it.

- Pace yourself. At the beginning of the exam, you will receive information about the questions or projects that are included in the exam. Some questions will require that you complete more than one task. Each project will require that you complete multiple tasks. During the exam, the amount of time remaining to complete the questions or project, and the number of completed and remaining questions if applicable, is shown at the bottom of the exam interface.

- Read the exam instructions carefully before beginning. Follow all the instructions provided completely and accurately.

- Enter requested information as it appears in the instructions, but without duplicating the formatting unless you are specifically instructed to do so. For example, the text and values you are asked to enter might appear in the instructions in bold and underlined text, but you should enter the information without applying these formats.

- Close all dialog boxes before proceeding to the next exam question unless you are specifically instructed not to do so.

- Don't close task panes before proceeding to the next exam question unless you are specifically instructed to do so.

- If you are asked to print a document, worksheet, chart, report, or slide, perform the task, but be aware that nothing will actually be printed.

- When performing tasks to complete a project-based exam, save your work frequently.

- Don't worry about extra keystrokes or mouse clicks. Your work is scored based on its result, not on the method you use to achieve that result (unless a specific method is indicated in the instructions).

- If a computer problem occurs during the exam (for example, if the exam does not respond or the mouse no longer functions) or if a power outage occurs, contact a testing center administrator immediately. The administrator will restart the computer and return the exam to the point where the interruption occurred, with your score intact.

> **Strategy** This book includes special tips for effectively studying for the Microsoft Office Specialist exams in Strategy paragraphs such as this one.

Certification benefits

At the conclusion of the exam, you will receive a score report, indicating whether you passed the exam. If your score meets or exceeds the passing standard (the minimum required score), you will be contacted by email by the Microsoft Certification Program team. The email message you receive will include your Microsoft Certification ID and links to online resources, including the Microsoft Certified Professional site. On this site, you can download or order a printed certificate, create a virtual business card, order an ID card, view and share your certification transcript, access the Logo Builder, and access other useful and interesting resources, including special offers from Microsoft and affiliated companies.

Depending on the level of certification you achieve, you will qualify to display one of three logos on your business card and other personal promotional materials. These logos attest to the fact that you are proficient in the applications or cross-application skills necessary to achieve the certification.

Microsoft
Office Specialist

Microsoft
Office Specialist Expert

Microsoft
Office Specialist Master

Using the Logo Builder, you can create a personalized certification logo that includes the MOS logo and the specific programs in which you have achieved certification. If you achieve MOS certification in multiple programs, you can include multiple certifications in one logo.

For more information

To learn more about the Microsoft Office Specialist exams and related courseware, visit:

http://www.microsoft.com/learning/en/us/mos-certification.aspx

Exams 77-427 and 77-428

Microsoft Excel 2013 Expert

This book covers the skills you need to have for certification as a Microsoft Office Specialist Expert in Microsoft Excel 2013. Specifically, you will need to be able to complete tasks that demonstrate the following skills:

1 Manage and share workbooks

2 Apply custom formats and layouts

3 Create advanced formulas

4 Create advanced charts and tables

With these skills, you can manage, format, populate, and enhance the type of workbooks most commonly used in business environments.

Prerequisites

We assume that you have been working with Excel 2013 for at least six months and that you know how to carry out fundamental tasks that are not specifically mentioned in the objectives for this Microsoft Office Specialist exam. This level of proficiency includes familiarity with features and tasks such as the following:

- Creating workbooks and using templates
- Adding worksheets to existing workbooks

- Copying and moving worksheets
- Inserting and deleting cells, columns, and rows
- Customizing the Quick Access Toolbar and the ribbon
- Recording simple macros
- Freezing panes and splitting the window
- Setting a print area and adding headers and footers
- Changing fonts and cell styles
- Wrapping text within cells
- Applying number formats and conditional formatting
- Creating named cells and ranges
- Creating and editing tables
- Using relative, mixed, and absolute cell references
- Using functions
- Creating and editing charts, and adding data series
- Inserting text boxes, SmartArt, and other images
- Applying styles and effects to objects
- Positioning objects

> **See Also** For information about the prerequisite tasks, see *MOS 2013 Study Guide for Microsoft Excel* by Joan Lambert (Microsoft Press, 2013).

1 Manage and share workbooks

The skills tested in this section of the Microsoft Office Specialist Expert exams for Microsoft Excel 2013 relate to advanced workbook management. Specifically, the following objectives are associated with this set of skills:

1.1 Manage multiple workbooks

1.2 Prepare workbooks for review

1.3 Manage workbook changes

In Excel 2013, you can set up separate workbooks to be maintained by multiple users, or you can set up a single workbook to be shared and edited by a group of users simultaneously.

This chapter guides you in studying methods for setting up and maintaining workbooks intended for sharing, distribution, and data collection; using properties to identify and organize workbooks; and ways to share a workbook so that you can track and review multiple users' changes, handle conflicts, and merge changes into a master workbook. Although the chapter focuses mainly on using workbooks in groups, many of these skills can be applied to solitary tasks.

> **Practice Files** To complete the practice tasks in this chapter, you need the practice files contained in the MOSExcel2013Expert\Objective1 practice file folder. For more information, see "Download the practice files" in this book's Introduction.

1.1 Manage multiple workbooks

Most Excel users have or will create more than one workbook for their own use, at work or at home. No one else sees the workbooks, so they don't have to be pretty or even particularly well organized. But to share workbooks with others, organize large data sets, or work with similar data from multiple sources, the techniques described in this section can be helpful in creating a manageable workflow.

Modifying workbook templates

Templates are featured prominently in the Backstage view (which you display by clicking the File tab). Excel has always included templates, but for Excel 2013, Microsoft invested considerable time and energy creating many new and sophisticated tools that are useful and visually appealing.

> **Tip** On the New page of the Backstage view, double-click a template thumbnail to bypass the preview window.

Use the Search For Online Templates box to find what's available. You might discover something useful and more sophisticated than you were planning to build, or learn some tricks that you can apply to your own creations. The library of available cloud-based templates is constantly updated and growing. For example, searching for "home inventory" finds, among other templates, a Home Inventory workbook that contains a table with slicer buttons.

> **Tip** Introduced in Excel 2010, slicers were only available for use with PivotTables, but are also available for use with tables in Excel 2013.

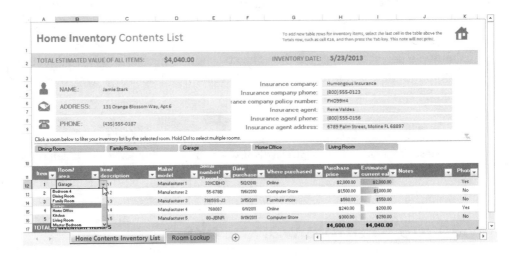

> **Tip** The Room/area column in the Home Inventory template includes drop-down lists that were created using the List option of the Data Validation command (Data tab). When you click new Room/area options in the lists, the table slicers change accordingly; more slicers are added as you add more unique categories to the table.

When you search for a template, try to find one that is as close to what you want as possible so you don't have to do a lot of editing beyond tasks such as adding a title, table headings, category names, and other minor tasks.

After you finalize a template, it can be used to create identical workbooks that can be used to collect and compile information from everyone on your distribution list.

> **Tip** After you save a template of your own, the Personal category appears as an option beneath the Search box on the New page, right next to the Featured category.
>
> You can change the default folder used to store custom templates on the Save page of the Excel Options dialog box, which defaults to C:\Users*user name*\My Documents\ Custom Office Templates.

> ➤ **To create a workbook from an online template**

1. On the **New** page of the **Backstage** view, enter a search term or phrase in the **Search for online templates** box.

2. In the search results, double-click the thumbnail image of the template you want to use.

➤ **To save a workbook as a template**

1. In the **Backstage** view, click the **Save** button, or if the file has already been saved, click **Save As**.

2. Click **Excel Template (*.xltx)** or **Excel Macro-Enabled Template (*.xltm)** in the **Save as type** list.

Managing workbook versions

Sometimes you need a do-over. The AutoRecover feature is normally turned on; when it is, you can retrieve versions of a workbook saved during the current session. On the Info page of the Backstage view, the available versions appear adjacent to the Manage Versions button.

Clicking one of the versions opens it as a separate workbook. Clicking the Manage Versions button displays a menu that contains the command Recover Unsaved Workbooks and, optionally, Delete All Unsaved Workbooks.

➤ **To turn on AutoRecover**

1. In the **Backstage view**, click **Options**.

2. In the **Excel Options** dialog box, display the **Save** page.

3. Make sure that the **Save AutoRecover information every <10> minutes** check box is selected. Adjust the frequency if you want, and then click **OK**.

➤ **To recover a previous version of a saved workbook**

1. On the **Info** page of the **Backstage view**, select the version of the file you want to restore.

2. Click the **Restore** button that appears in the yellow alert area at the top of the workbook to overwrite the newer version with the restored version, or close the restored workbook without saving.

➤ **To recover a previous version of an unsaved workbook**

1. On the **Info** page, click the **Manage Versions** button, and then click **Recover Unsaved Workbooks**.

2. In the **Open** dialog box, select the file name, and then click **OK**.

> **Strategy** The objective domain for Exam 77-428 includes "Merging multiple workbooks," under Objective 1.1. This relies on the Share Workbook command, which is discussed in section 1.2, "Prepare workbooks for review," which also covers shared workbooks and change tracking. Merging workbooks is discussed in section 1.3, "Manage workbook changes," later in this chapter.

Copying styles between templates

Cell styles that you create can be saved as custom styles and transferred to other workbooks or templates. New styles are added to the Custom category, which appears on the Cell Styles menu only when the workbook contains custom cell styles.

Merging styles that have the same name

When you use the Merge Styles command, you might see a dialog box that asks you to decide whether to merge styles that have the same names into the active workbook. The term "merging" can imply otherwise, but in this case, to merge is to overwrite. Styles in the source workbook will replace styles with the same names in the destination workbook. Here are some things to consider:

- In Excel, and in other Office applications, unspecified fonts and colors are controlled by themes.

- A style might look different when a different theme is applied.

- Themes are shared among Office applications.

If you work with multiple themes, avoid merging same-named styles. If you don't use themes, or the workbooks already share a common theme, it probably doesn't matter if you overwrite same-named styles. However, if you only want to copy your custom styles, just say No to merging styles with the same name.

➤ **To copy styles between workbooks**

1. Open the source and destination workbooks.

2. In the destination workbook, in the **Styles** group on the **Home** tab, click **Cell Styles**, and then click **Merge Styles**.

3. In the **Merge Styles** dialog box, select the source workbook. Then click **OK**.

4. If the **Merge styles that have the same names?** message appears, click **Yes** if you want to overwrite styles in the destination workbook, or click **No** if you want to keep them.

> **Tip** In Excel, when you copy a styled cell or range from one workbook or template to another, the formatting will transfer, but the style will neither transfer nor appear in the Styles palette.

Copying macros between workbooks

Macros are sequences of actions captured by using the Record Macro command, or snippets of handwritten code, which are used to complete repetitive tasks or complex procedures. Macros are recorded as Microsoft Visual Basic for Applications (VBA) code and are stored in modules. You use the Visual Basic Editor to edit macros and modules.

Unless you are comfortable working with VBA code, the safest and easiest way to copy macros from workbook to workbook is to copy the entire VBA module. But first, you need to make sure the Developer tab is visible on the ribbon.

> **Tip** You might need to change the macro security level to allow all of your macros to transfer properly. If you do so, be sure to turn macro security back on when you're done.

➤ **To display the Developer tab**

1. On the **Customize Ribbon** page of the **Excel Options** dialog box, select **Main Tabs** in the **Customize the Ribbon** list.

2. In the **Customize the Ribbon** pane, select the **Developer** check box. Then click **OK**.

➤ **To enable macros**

1. On the **Developer** tab, in the **Code** group, click **Macro Security**.

2. On the **Macro Settings** page of the **Trust Center** dialog box, click **Enable All Macros (not recommended; potentially dangerous code can run)**. Then click **OK**.

➤ **To copy a macro between workbooks**

1. Open both the source and destination workbooks.

2. On the **Developer** tab, click the **Visual Basic** button.

3. In the **Microsoft Visual Basic for Applications** window, in the **Project Explorer** pane (docked on the left side of the window), press **Ctrl**, and then drag the module (for example, *Module1*) located under **VBAProject** for the source workbook to **VBAProject** for the destination workbook.

4. Close the Visual Basic Editor and save the destination workbook.

Connecting to external data

When you connect to an external data source, Excel provides options to import the data into a PivotTable, a PivotTable with a PivotChart, a Power View report, or a table. When you set up the external data as a PivotTable (with or without a PivotChart), you can use tools such as a slicer to analyze the data.

> **See Also** For more information about creating and working with PivotTables and PivotCharts, including how to apply a slicer to a PivotTable, see section 4.2, "Create and manage PivotTables," and section 4.3, "Create and manage PivotCharts."

You work with two groups of commands on the Data tab to create and manage connections to data sources outside an Excel workbook. With the Get External Data group of commands, you can make quick connections to common sources. Use the Connections group commands to manage the connections you create.

> **Tip** Excel Services is a service application that you can use to work with Excel workbooks on Microsoft SharePoint.

About the Excel Data Model

No matter what method you use to import external data, you will eventually arrive at the Import Data dialog box. The last check box in the Import Data dialog box is the cryptic Add This Data To The Data Model. New in 2013, the Data Model allows you to analyze disparate data sources in the same workbook, allowing pseudo-relational database functionality by using multiple tables. By incorporating your data into the Data Model, you can analyze more than one table at a time by using PivotTables, PivotCharts, PowerPivot, and Power View Reports. (PowerPivot and Power View are available only with certain premium configurations of Microsoft Office.) You can add more tables to the Data Model, from Microsoft Access databases, websites, SQL Server tables, other workbooks, and text files. Excel collects data from all the tables that have been added to the Data Model, allowing you to build relationships among them, similar to relational database programs. For more information, see section 4.2, "Create and manage PivotTables."

The commands available on the Get External Data menu provide different paths to the same objective. Here are some of the things you'll need to know in order to use these commands:

- **From Access** Provide the name and location of a database, select a database object (a table or a query defined in the database), and specify how you want the data to be presented in Excel.

- **From Web** To set properties for web queries, you work in the External Data Range Properties dialog box; specify data-refreshment options and formatting.

- **From Text** Connect to a text file (a file that uses the .txt, .csv, or .prn file name extension), and Excel starts the Text Import Wizard. Specify how to import the data, delimited or fixed-width columns, the starting row, and optionally apply basic formats to each column.

- **From Other Sources** For most of these sources, you'll need server name and logon information. The following list provides additional details about other connection types on the menu:

  - **From Data Connection Wizard** A variety of data sources is available, including Windows Azure Marketplace, SQL Server, and SQL Server Analysis Services. If you work with Oracle databases, use Microsoft Data Access – OLE DB Provider for Oracle. The Other/Advanced data source opens the Data Link Properties dialog box, offering a list of Microsoft OLE DB providers.

  - **From SQL Server** Use the Data Connection Wizard to select the database, and optionally connect to a specific table.

  - **From XML Data Import** To see the structure of the XML file, switch to the Developer tab and then click Source in the XML group.

  - **From Microsoft Query** You can use Microsoft Query to connect to an Access database, a SQL Server database, an OLAP cube, or another Excel file. You can also use Microsoft Query to define a new data source.

- **Existing Connections** Any connections already defined in the current workbook, on your computer, or on your network are listed here. Select a connection and then click Open to add it to the current workbook.

To manage connections to the current workbook only, click Connections on the Data tab to display the Workbook Connections dialog box, where you can add or remove connections, set connection properties, and refresh the data in specific connections or in all connections. Follow the directions at the bottom of the dialog box to see where the connections are used.

Editing formula links

You can create individual linking formulas that rely on data from other workbooks, such as the formula ='Alpine-Sales.xlsx'!jan2014sales, which refers to a cell named jan2014sales in an open workbook named Alpine-Sales. (If the workbook were closed, the formula would also include the full path to the workbook.) While the source workbooks are available (open or not), using external references keeps data from other sources current without having to update manually. To manage external references, click Edit Links on the Data tab where you can open, change, update, break, or check the status of links. You can also have Excel display a dialog box each time a workbook is opened that asks whether or not to update links, or to update them without asking.

➤ **To get data from an Access database**

1. On the **Data** tab, click **Get External Data**, and then click **From Access**.

2. In the **Select Data Source** dialog box, locate and select your database, and then click **Open**.

3. In the **Select Table** dialog box, select the database object (table or query) that contains the data you need, and then click **OK**.

4. In the **Import Data** dialog box, choose how you want the data to be presented and where it should be placed, or click **New worksheet**. If you plan to add more tables, click **Add this data to the Data Model**.

5. In the **Import Data** dialog box, click **Properties**.

6. In the **Connection Properties** dialog box, enter a connection name and description, set the refresh control, and adjust other properties as needed.

7. Click **OK** twice to close the **Connection Properties** and **Import Data** dialog boxes.

➤ **To get data from a web-based source**

1. On the **Data** tab, click **Get External Data**, and then click **From Web**.

2. In the **New Web Query** dialog box, in the **Address** box, enter a URL.

3. Click the arrow icons adjacent to the tables you want to select on the webpage (they change to selected check boxes when clicked), and then click **Import**.

4. In the **Import Data** dialog box, specify where to place the data or click **New worksheet**.

5. In the **Import Data** dialog box, click **Properties**.

6. In the **External Data Range Properties** dialog box, enter a connection name and set other options as needed.

7. Click **OK** twice to close the **External Data Range Properties** and **Import Data** dialog boxes.

➤ **To get data from a text file**

1. On the **Data** tab, click **Get External Data**, and then click **From Text**.

2. In the **Import Text File** dialog box, select the file you want to import, and then click **Import**.

3. On the first page of the **Text Import Wizard**, click **Delimited** or **Fixed width** depending on how the data is organized in the text file, and then click **Next**.

4. On the second page of the wizard, specify the delimiting character if you chose Delimited in the previous step, or specify column breaks if you selected Fixed Width. Then click **Next**.

5. On the third page of the wizard, change the data format for any columns (if required) and select any columns you want to skip. Then click **Finish**.

6. In the **Import Data** dialog box, specify where to place the data or click **New worksheet**.

7. In the **Import Data** dialog box, click **Properties**.

8. In the **External Data Range Properties** dialog box, enter a connection name and set other options as needed.

9. Click **OK** twice to close the **External Data Range Properties** and **Import Data** dialog boxes.

➤ **To open an existing connection**

1. On the **Data** tab, click **Get External Data**, and then click **Existing Connections**.

2. In the **Existing Connections** dialog box, select a connection, and then click **Open**.

3. In the **Import Data** dialog box, select appropriate view and placement options, and then click **OK**.

➤ **To make a worksheet available to Excel Services**

1. In the **Import Data** dialog box, click **Properties**.

2. In the **Connection Properties** dialog box, click **Authentication Settings**.

3. Specify the type of authentication required for users to access this data.

4. To use this connection on a different computer, click **Export Connection File**.

➤ **To add a workbook connection**

1. On the **Data** tab, click **Connections**.

2. In the **Workbook Connections** dialog box, click **Add**.

➤ **To remove or refresh a workbook connection**

1. On the **Data** tab, click **Connections**.

2. Select a connection, and then click **Remove** or **Refresh**.

➤ **To view workbook connection properties**

→ On the **Data** tab, click **Properties**.

➤ **To update external references**

→ On the **Data** tab, click **Edit Links**, and then click **Update Values**.

➤ **To manage external references**

→ On the **Data** tab, click **Edit Links**, and then click **Change Source**.

➤ **To open an external reference source**

→ On the **Data** tab, click **Edit Links**, and then click **Open Source**.

➤ **To break an external reference link**

→ On the **Data** tab, click **Edit Links**, and then click **Break Link**.

➤ **To check the status of external references**

→ On the **Data** tab, click **Edit Links**, and then click **Check Status**.

➤ **To display a startup prompt when updating external references**

→ On the **Data** tab, click **Edit Links**, and then click **Startup Prompt** and specify whether Excel displays an alert when opening the workbook, and whether links are updated automatically.

Practice tasks

The practice files for these tasks are located in the MOSExcel2013Expert\Objective1 practice file folder. Save the results of the tasks in the same folder.

- Open the *ExcelExpert_1-1a* template, modify it, and save it as a new template.

- Open a new workbook and import data from the *ExcelExpert_1-1b* database.

- Open the *ExcelExpert_1-1c* workbook, click Don't Update in the dialog box that appears, and then use the Edit Links command to change the links in *ExcelExpert_1-1c* so that they point to *ExcelExpert_1-1d*.

1.2 Prepare workbooks for review

If you need to share a workbook with one or more co-workers in order to collect comments, updates, changes, and suggestions, you'll probably need to use more than just the obvious feature: change tracking. You should consider what is or isn't discoverable in a document's properties (metadata). You might consider using protection features in Excel to restrict editing to specific cells. You might want to restrict changes to worksheet structure, control recalculation, or add password protection.

This section describes techniques and considerations when setting up a workbook for optimal data collection, before you send it out for review.

Tracking changes

When you activate change tracking, Excel records and saves most of the edits performed in a workbook, from session to session, for minutes to months, until you turn change tracking off. The Excel command you need for change tracking is Highlight Changes, located on the Track Changes menu on the Review tab.

Setting tracking options

You can set change tracking options in two ways in the Changes group on the Review tab:

- Click the Share Workbook button. Then in the Share Workbook dialog box, you can select the Allow Changes By More Than One User check box to activate options on the Advanced page of the dialog box, including the number of days to keep the change history, how often to update changes (from only when saved to every five minutes), how to resolve conflicting changes, and whether to control print and filter settings.

- On the Track Changes menu, click Highlight Changes to set additional tracking options. In the Highlight Changes dialog box, click Track Changes While Editing, and then select options in the When, Who, and Where lists. The Who list offers the static options Everyone and Everyone But Me, and also lists the names of all others with whom the workbook is shared. You can use the options in the Where box to limit the highlight changes to a specific cell range by entering a range address, or by dragging to select the range directly on the worksheet.

Highlight Changes ? ×

☑ Track changes while editing. This also shares your workbook.

Highlight which changes

☑ When: All

☑ Who: Everyone

☐ Where:

☑ Highlight changes on screen

☐ List changes on a new sheet

OK

Photo?	Price	Quantity	Total
	$25.00		Mark Dodge, 5/23/2013 4:13 PM: Changed cell I10 from '$0.00' to '$25.00'.
	$21.00		
	$33.00		
	$112.00	11	$1,232.00
	$233.00	2	$466.00
	$566.00	1	$566.00
	$39.00	18	$702.00
	$19.00	22	$418.00
	$112.00	1	$112.00
	$19.00	12	$228.00
	$1.00	57	$57.00

> **Tip** Sharing and change tracking features will not work if the workbook contains Excel tables. You can convert tables to normal ranges while preserving formatting and formulas by clicking any cell in the table and then clicking Convert To Range in the Tools group on the Design tool tab. If you do so, formulas and defined names might require adjustment.

Excel tracks most substantive changes to worksheet content. Excluded are changes to sheet names and formatting, adding or changing comments, changes resulting from recalculation, unsaved changes, and inserted or deleted sheets. Edits made to inserted sheets are tracked, however. Although Excel does not restore a deleted sheet or remove an inserted sheet if you reject such tracked edits, Excel does record the acts of insertion or deletion in the change history log.

> **Tip** In Excel, activating change tracking also activates workbook sharing, allowing multiple editors to work on shared copies of the workbook.

As soon as you turn off change tracking, Excel discards the change history log, and this can't be undone. This is true for each shared workbook copy that you distribute. To prevent the loss of valuable data, you can prevent anyone but the owner of the master workbook from turning off change tracking. Reviewers normally can't turn off change tracking; however, they can turn off sharing for their copy of the workbook. Adding a password prevents unauthorized reviewers from turning off either tracking or sharing.

> **Tip** You can protect your change history log by clicking List Changes On A New Sheet in the Highlight Changes dialog box, which places a copy of the log on a new worksheet.

➤ **To turn on change tracking**

1. On the **Review** tab, in the **Changes** group, click **Track Changes**, and then click **Highlight Changes**.

2. In the **Highlight Changes** dialog box, select the **Track changes while editing** check box.

3. Select options in the **When** and **Who** lists.

4. To select specific cells or ranges in which you want to track changes, click **Where**, and then make your selection. Changes to other cells are ignored.

5. Click **OK** to close the dialog box, and then click **OK** in the dialog box notifying you that the workbook will be saved. (Note that your tracking option changes are not saved if you decline to save the workbook at this point.)

➤ **To configure tracking options**

1. On the **Review** tab, in the **Changes** group, click **Share Workbook**.

2. In the **Share Workbook** dialog box, on the **Editing** page, select the **Allow changes by more than one user...** check box.

3. On the **Advanced** page, select from the four categories which options you want, and then click **OK**.

4. In the Excel warning dialog box, click **OK** to save the workbook and your sharing changes.

5. On the **Review** tab, in the **Changes** group, click **Track Changes**, and then click **Highlight Changes**.

6. In the **Highlight Changes** dialog box, click **Track changes while editing**.

7. If you want, select and make changes in the **When** and **Who** lists, and select specific cells to track in the **Where** edit box.

➤ **To insert the change history log on a new worksheet**

1. On the **Review** tab, in the **Changes** group, click **Track Changes**, and then click **Highlight Changes**.

2. In the **Highlight Changes** dialog box, click **All** in the **When** list.

3. Click **List changes on a new sheet**, and then click **OK**.

➤ **To stop tracking changes**

1. On the **Review** tab, in the **Changes** group, click **Track Changes**, and then click **Highlight Changes**.

2. In the **Highlight Changes** dialog box, clear the **Track Changes While Editing. This Also Shares your Workbook** check box. (Note that if the workbook is protected, you must unprotect it before turning off change tracking.)

> **Strategy** The objective domain for Exam 77-428 includes "Opening workspaces," in the Objective 1.2 section. This refers to a feature that was removed in Excel 2013. You can open an old workspace file (.xlw), which continues to open any associated files, but you cannot save any new workspaces.

Protecting workbooks for sharing

Protection is a multifaceted process in Excel. You can apply protection "formatting" to individual cells and ranges. You can protect individual worksheets and almost everything they might contain. You can protect the workbook from any structural modifications. And, of course, you can require a password to open the file itself. When you are planning to share a workbook for review, you can use protection features to allow editing to specific cells, and to protect everything else. You can also restrict access if you have a Rights Management Server available.

Restricting editing and limiting editors

On a fresh, unprotected worksheet, you can enter anything anywhere, even though all cells are considered locked by default. This is so that, when you finally activate sheet protection, all cells are covered except for those you specifically choose to unlock. But so-called locked cells are still editable until you do activate sheet protection. Because every cell on a fresh worksheet is locked by default, you need to unlock cells in order to make them available for editing when protection is in force. On the Home tab, the Lock Cell command on the Format menu is a toggle—click off/click on. The padlock icon appears "boxed" when a selected cell or range is locked.

> **Tip** If you plan to share a workbook containing formulas that you want to hide from view, you can use a special format to do so. Click Format on the Home tab and click Format Cells (or just press Ctrl+1) to open the Format Cells dialog box. On the Protection tab, click Hidden to hide formulas in selected cells.

After you unlock your editable cells, you need to protect the sheet to begin restricting editing. The Protect Sheet dialog box lists actions you can allow, with Select Locked Cells and Select Unlocked Cells selected by default. Note, however, that most of the actions listed cannot be change-tracked.

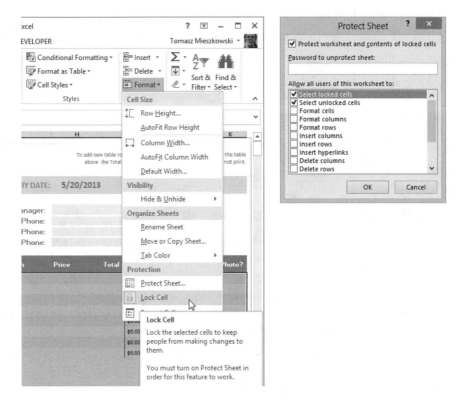

With the worksheet protected, only the cells unlocked by using the Lock Cell command can be edited. In fact, locking the sheet makes editing a little bit easier, because pressing the Tab key in a locked sheet activates the next unlocked cell. Because all locked cells are skipped, you can just make an entry and then press Tab to both accept the entry and activate the next cell available to edit. Note, however, that you or anyone else can unlock the sheet unless you add a password by using the Password To Unprotect Sheet box in the Protect Sheet dialog box.

Excel also provides the Allow Users To Edit Ranges command on the Review tab, which provides capabilities beyond using the technique of locking cells and protecting sheets. Although this command does essentially the same thing, it makes it easier to keep track of the ranges you specify, and allows you to set a separate password for each range. You can also apply permissions to each range, if you are working within a domain that provides access control.

> ### To restrict editing

1. Select only the cells that you want reviewers to edit.

2. On the **Home** tab, in the **Cells** group, click **Format**, and then click **Lock Cell**.

3. On the **Review** tab, in the **Changes** group, click **Protect Sheet**.

4. Select the **Protect Worksheet and Contents of Locked Cells** check box.

5. Enter a password, if desired.

6. In the **Allow All Users of the Worksheet To** list, select any additional actions that you want to allow, and then click **OK** to close the dialog box.

> ### To remove editing restrictions

→ On the **Home** tab, in the **Cells** group, click **Format**, and then click **Unprotect Sheet**, and provide a password, if necessary.

> ### To limit editors for selected cells

1. Select the cells or ranges in which you want to allow editing.

2. On the **Review** tab, in the **Changes** group, click **Allow Users to Edit Ranges**.

3. In the **Allow Users to Edit Ranges** dialog box, click the **New** button.

4. Enter a name for your range in the **Title** box.

5. Enter a password to edit the range if you want, and click **OK**.

6. Click the **Permissions** button.

7. Select each group or user name to whom you want to grant editing privileges, and click the **Add** button.

8. For each editor added, click either **Allow** or **Deny**.

9. Close both the **Permissions** and **New Range** dialog boxes by clicking **OK**.

10. In the **Allow Users to Edit Ranges** dialog box, click **OK** to apply the changes and close the dialog box.

Or

Click the **Apply** button to add the current range to the list, keeping the dialog box open to add more ranges. Then click **OK** when finished.

Protecting worksheet structure

When you are finished specifying protection and editing options, choose the Protect Workbook command. The default option (Structure) prevents users from adding or deleting worksheets, displaying source data for PivotTable reports, running macros that try to perform prohibited actions, or creating a Scenario Summary report or any other action that closes, hides, or creates a new worksheet. Clicking the Windows option prevents users from changing the size or location of worksheet windows (however, users can still hide and unhide them).

> **Tip** Much of the functionality of the Windows protection option was curtailed with the implementation of the Single Document Interface in Excel 2013 (wherein each open workbook and window creates separate instances of Excel). The Save Workspace command was removed in 2013 for the same reason.

➤ **To protect the structure of a workbook**

1. On the **Info** page of the **Backstage view**, click **Protect Workbook**, and then click **Protect Workbook Structure**.

Or

On the **Review** tab, in the **Changes** group, click **Protect Workbook**.

2. In the **Protect Structure and Windows** dialog box, select the options you want, enter an optional password, and then click **OK**.

➤ **To protect the current worksheet**

1. On the **Info** page, click **Protect Workbook**, and then click **Protect Current Sheet**.

Or

On the **Review** tab, in the **Changes** group, click **Protect Sheet**.

2. In the **Protect Sheet** dialog box, select the operations you want to allow users to perform. **Select Locked Cells** and **Select Unlocked Cells** are selected by default.

3. Enter a password that allows you to remove sheet protection, and then click **OK**.

> **To protect and share a workbook**

1. On the **Review** tab, in the **Changes** group, click **Protect and Share Workbook** (or **Protect Shared Workbook** if the workbook is already shared) to open the **Protect Shared Workbook** dialog box.

2. Click **Sharing with track changes**.

3. Enter a password if you want.

4. Click **OK** to close the dialog box, and again in the warning message to save the workbook and your sharing choices.

Removing workbook metadata

Metadata is information attached to a document that is independent of the data contained within. It often includes sensitive information, including author and reviewer names, file and printer paths, and custom XML data. So, it's a good idea to clean up your workbooks before you disseminate them. Happily, Excel makes this easy. When you inspect a document, Excel reports what it finds and allows you to choose the issues to resolve.

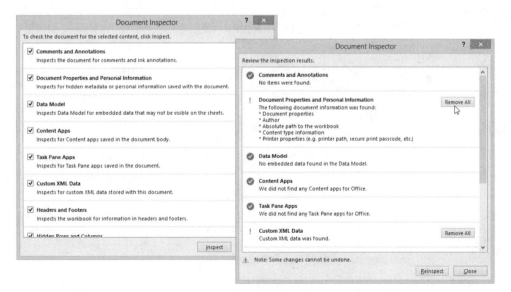

The Document Inspector includes 20 categories of metadata, all of which are normally selected. You can deselect any category you don't want inspected, and then click the Inspect button to display the results (nothing is deleted yet). After you click Inspect, the Document Inspector displays results for each category of metadata, and offers a Remove All button you can use to clean up that category.

Properties vs. metadata

When you create and edit a workbook, Excel records properties about the workbook such as the file size, the created and last modified dates, and the name of the workbook's author. These non-editable properties are displayed on the Info page of the Backstage view, along with a few editable ones with labels. More options are available if you click the Properties heading on the Info page and click Advanced Properties.

All workbook properties are considered metadata (also known as "data about data"). Metadata is employed to organize other data, and used in cataloging and searching for documents, but metadata often represents a security risk when sharing.

➤ **To inspect a workbook**

1. On the **Info** page of the **Backstage** view, click **Check for Issues**, and then click **Inspect Document**.

2. In the **Document Inspector** dialog box, clear the check boxes for any content areas you don't want to inspect.

3. Click **Inspect**.

4. Review the inspection results that Excel displays. Click **Remove All** if you want Excel to clear up that area of the workbook for you. Otherwise, click **Close**, manually address the issues raised, and then reinspect the document.

See Also For information about inspecting documents for compatibility and accessibility, see section 2.4, "Prepare a workbook for internationalization and accessibility."

Controlling calculation

Workbook calculation is the process Excel uses to compute formulas and display the results as values, which is usually automatic. Excel updates values each time you enter or change data in a workbook. To avoid unnecessary calculations, Excel automatically recalculates formulas only when the cells that the formula depends on change. Manual calculation might come in handy when you're working with a large number of formulas or links. To change workbook calculation options, in the Excel Options dialog box, display the Formulas page and choose options in the Calculation Options section.

The Formulas tab on the ribbon also includes two commands you can use to perform manual calculation:

- Calculate Now calculates formulas in the whole workbook.
- Calculate Sheet updates the formulas in the current worksheet.

Most users of Excel have mistakenly (or deliberately) entered a formula that creates a circular reference, which occurs when you refer to a cell in a formula that refers back to the cell containing the formula. For example, the formula =A1*B1 entered in cell B1 creates a circular reference. Most of the time, circular references can be resolved by moving the formula to a different cell. Some calculations, however, depend on circular references. For example, IF statements that are used to specify conditions in a formula can result in circular references. To resolve these references, click the Enable Iterative Calculation option on the Formulas page of the Excel Options dialog box.

> **See Also** For information about the IF function, see section 3.1, "Apply functions in formulas."

> **Tip** You can also access some of these options by clicking the Calculation Options button in the Calculation group on the Formulas tab. Clicking Calculation Options displays three of the same settings included in the Excel Options dialog box.

In an iterative calculation, Excel recalculates a worksheet until a specific numeric condition is met. If a formula refers back to one of its own cells, you must determine how many times the formula should be recalculated. Circular references can iterate indefinitely; however, you can control the maximum number of iterations (which affects how many times Excel calculates the worksheet) and the amount of acceptable change. Excel stops recalculating the worksheet if the maximum change from one iteration to the next is less than the value specified in the Maximum Change field (which is 0.001 by default). Reduce the Maximum Change setting to a smaller number (0.000001, for example) if you need to make calculations that require greater precision.

Iteration comes into play also when you use the Excel Solver or the Goal Seek command for performing a what-if analysis. Both commands use iterative calculations to obtain results that reflect criteria that you define. You can use the Excel Solver when you need to find the optimum value for a particular cell by adjusting the values of several cells or when you want to apply specific limitations to one or more of the values in the calculation. You can use the Goal Seek command when you know the result you want for a single formula but not the values the formula needs to get the result you want.

> **See Also** For more information about the Solver and Goal Seek commands, see section 3.4, "Create scenarios."

> ➤ **To change workbook calculation options**

1. In the **Backstage view**, click **Options**.

2. In the **Excel Options** dialog box, display the **Formulas** page.

3. Select the options you want, and then click **OK**.

> ➤ **To calculate the current worksheet**

➜ Click the **Formulas** tab, and then in the **Calculation group**, click **Calculate Sheet**.

> ➤ **To calculate the current workbook**

➜ Click the **Formulas** tab, and then in the **Calculation** group, click **Calculate Now**.

> ➤ **To set the maximum number of iterations**

1. In the **Backstage view**, click **Options**.

2. In the **Excel Options** dialog box, on the **Formulas** page, select **Enable iterative calculation**.

3. In the **Maximum Iterations** box, set the maximum number of times Excel should perform a recalculation.

4. In the **Maximum Change** box, specify the maximum amount of change to accept between recalculation results, and then click **OK**.

Encrypting workbooks by using a password

Excel provides several types of password protection, and offers encryption. Both methods use passwords, but where password-protecting document files prevents their opening, encryption additionally protects the contents of the document. Available third-party tools can access data from password-protected documents without even having to open them.

Important Take heed of the warning in the Encrypt Document dialog box about lost passwords; they can't be recovered. Be sure to record the password in a safe place.

Tip Not all file formats that Excel can read are compatible with passwords. For example, files stored in the .csv format do not accept a password. Excel might not let you know if it doesn't work, however, so check the file after applying a password.

➤ **To encrypt a file with a password**

   1. On the **Info** page of the **Backstage view**, click **Protect Workbook**, and then click **Encrypt with Password**.

   2. In the **Encrypt Document** dialog box, enter a password, and then click **OK**.

   3. Reenter the password.

   4. Click **OK**, and then save the workbook.

➤ **To remove password encryption**

   1. On the **Info** page, click **Protect Workbook**, and then click **Encrypt with Password**.

   2. In the **Encrypt Document** dialog box, delete the password.

   3. Click **OK**, and then save the workbook.

➤ **To password-protect a file**

   1. In the **Backstage view**, click **Save As** and select a destination folder.

   2. In the **Save As** dialog box, click the **Tools** menu, and then click **General Options**.

   3. Enter a password in the **Password to Open** box.

   4. Optionally, enter a password in the **Password to Modify** box and/or click the **Always Create Backup** option.

   5. Click **OK** to close the dialog box.

Marking as final

To communicate to your co-workers that you have finished with a workbook, you can use the Mark As Final command, a useful tool for job tracking and record keeping. When you mark a workbook as final, it is immediately saved as read-only, the Status property of the document is set to "Final," typing is disabled, all proofing and editing commands are disabled, a message bar appears above the worksheet displaying an "Edit Anyway" button, and an indicator appears in the Status bar. If these indicators ever disappear after marking a workbook as final, you know that it has been edited.

If you would prefer to tell reviewers that a workbook is still in progress, but not for editing, you can do so by using a gentle hint from the Read-Only Recommended feature. This feature displays a message whenever a workbook is opened, suggesting that it be opened in read-only mode, and offers a helpful button with which to do so.

It should be noted that neither of these features provide actual security. Users can decline the suggestion to open the workbook as read-only, and anyone can turn off Mark As Final.

> **To save a workbook as read-only recommended**

1. In the **Backstage view**, click **Save As** and select a destination folder.

2. In the **Save As** dialog box, click the **Tools** menu, and then click **General Options**.

3. Select the **Read-Only Recommended** check box, and then click **OK**.

> **To mark a workbook as final**

1. On the **Info** page of the **Backstage view**, click the **Protect Workbook** button, and then click **Mark as Final**.

2. Click **OK** in the warning message box explaining that the workbook will be marked as final and saved. Then click **OK** in the information message box that explains the limitations placed on a marked-as-final workbook.

Practice tasks

The practice file for this task is located in the MOSExcel2013Expert\Objective1 practice file folder. Save the results of the tasks in the same folder.

- Open the *ExcelExpert_1-2* workbook, and try the following tasks:
    - ○ Restrict editing to the cells in the Units column.
    - ○ Restrict editing and require a password to edit the cells in the Price column.
    - ○ Instigate change tracking. Then protect and share the workbook.
    - ○ If possible, distribute copies to other Excel users.
    - ○ Enter data into the input cells. Then review and accept changes.
    - ○ Encrypt the workbook with a password.
    - ○ Remove metadata and mark the workbook as final.

1.3 Manage workbook changes

Excel provides a good mechanism for collecting, adjudicating, and summarizing input from multiple co-workers. The previous section described how to initiate change tracking and distribute copies of a shared workbook to reviewers. This section explains what to do with all those changes, plus some other tools you can use to identify errors and resolve problems that can arise.

Displaying all changes

The first time you open an edited workbook in which the changes have been tracked, you might see no revision marks in evidence. In the Highlight Changes dialog box, the Since I Last Saved option is probably the culprit. For example, when editing a shared, change-tracked workbook, you might see revision marks appear on the worksheet as you work, but they disappear as soon as you save the workbook.

➤ **To display all tracked changes**

1. On the **Review** tab, in the **Changes** group, click **Track Changes**, and then click **Highlight Changes**.

2. In the **When** list, click **All**, and then click **OK**.

Reviewing changes

To review changes made to a shared workbook, click Track Changes on the Review tab, and then click Accept/Reject Changes. Excel saves the workbook after all changes have been reviewed and then displays a dialog box containing When, Who, and Where lists with slightly different options than those in the Highlight Changes dialog box. As you review changes, Excel displays a description of the change under review, including the date and time, who made it, and details about the changes made.

➤ **To retain or reject changes to a shared workbook**

1. On the **Review** tab, in the **Changes** group, click **Track Changes**, and then click **Accept/Reject Changes**.

2. In the **Select Changes to Accept or Reject** dialog box, specify which changes you want to review, and then click **OK**.

3. In the **Accept or Reject Changes** dialog box, move from revision to revision and accept or reject each one, or click either **Accept All** or **Reject All**.

Managing comments

Comments are notes you can add to cells in order to provide users with additional information, such as flagging corrections or questionable values. They can be used by workbook owners to provide documentation about how to use a workbook, or to provide explanations for data that is certain to raise questions.

The Comments group on the Review tab contains all the tools needed to add, edit, review, and control the display of comments. When you add a comment, a small triangle indicator appears in the upper-right corner of the cell. Otherwise, comments remain hidden until you either rest the mouse pointer over the cell or click the Show All Comments button on the Review tab.

> **To add a comment**

1. Select the cell to which you want to attach a comment.

2. On the **Review** tab, in the **Comments** group, click **New Comment**, and then enter your message.

> **To review comments**

→ In the **Comments** group, click the **Next** button or **Previous** button to display the next comment (even if none are selected).

> **To view all comments**

→ In the **Comments** group, click **Show All Comments**.

Merging workbooks

If you need a group of people to review a workbook, you can save it for sharing, distribute a copy of the workbook to each member of the group, collect the workbooks after changes are made, and then merge the changes into a single workbook. In order to merge changes, you must distribute copies of the same original workbook to all reviewers, and the workbook must be shared. In addition, all users of the shared workbook must:

- Save a copy of the original workbook with a unique file name (adding their own name to the file name, for example).

- Add their changes to their own copy of the original workbook.

- Save all the copies in the same folder as the original (or send them to the owner to place in the original folder).

> **Tip** When you merge workbooks, be sure that multiple reviewers are not editing the same cells; if so, you'll need to carefully review each merged workbook to ensure that the correct data is collected, and that subsequent reviewers' edits do not overwrite the data.

Before you begin, you need to add the Compare And Merge Workbooks command to the Quick Access Toolbar or to the ribbon. If you work with shared workbooks frequently, you might add this command to a custom group on the Review tab.

> **See Also** For more information about customizing the ribbon and the Quick Access Toolbar, see section 1.4, "Customize options and views for worksheets and workbooks" in *MOS 2013 Study Guide for Microsoft Excel* by Joan Lambert (Microsoft Press, 2013).

> **Tip** When you distribute separate copies of a workbook to a group, base the workbook on a template. For more information, see section 1.1, "Manage multiple workbooks."

To begin, open the original workbook that was used to make the distributed copies, then click Compare And Merge Workbooks. Select the first copy of the file you want to merge in the Select Files To Merge Into Current Workbook dialog box, click Open, and then repeat these steps for each version (or press Ctrl+click to select multiple files at once).

After you merge workbooks, you can display all changes, and accept or reject them, as you do with other shared workbooks.

> **See Also** For the steps you follow to review track changes, see "Reviewing Changes" earlier in this chapter.

➤ **To add the Compare and Merge Workbooks button to the Quick Access Toolbar**

1. In the **Backstage view**, click **Options**.

2. In the **Excel Options** dialog box, display the **Quick Access Toolbar** page.

3. In the **Choose Commands From** list, select **All Commands**.

4. In the commands list, select **Compare and Merge Workbooks**, and then click the **Add** button.

➤ **To set up your workbooks for distribution and merging**

1. Open the workbook you want to distribute.

2. On the **Review** tab, in the **Changes** group, click **Share Workbook**.

3. In the **Share Workbook** dialog box, on the **Editing** page, select the **Allow changes by more than one user at the same time** check box.

4. On the **Advanced** page, in the **Keep change history for** box, specify the time span that users have to review the file. Then click **OK** to save the shared workbook.

5. In the **Backstage** view, use the **Save As** command to create a separate copy of the workbook for each reviewer. Use the original workbook you shared as the master.

6. Pass out the copies to reviewers. Be sure to let them know when the files are expected back.

➤ **To merge changes**

1. Open the master shared workbook.

2. On the Quick Access Toolbar, click the **Compare and Merge Workbooks** button to display the **Select Files to Merge into Current Workbook** dialog box. (If the Merge And Compare Workbooks button is not visible, you'll need to add it to the Quick Access Toolbar.)

3. Select the files you want to merge, and then click **Open**.

4. On the **Review** tab, in the **Changes** group, click **Track Changes**, and then click **Accept/Reject Changes**.

5. In the **Accept or Reject Changes** dialog box, move from revision to revision and accept or reject each one, or click either **Accept All** or **Reject All**.

Identifying errors

Many formula errors are simple mistakes. For example, you might misplace or omit an opening or closing parenthesis, define a cell range without using a colon, or try to divide by zero. Excel quickly spots these types of errors and displays a message in a cell that contains an errant formula and offers to fix it. The following are error values that might appear in cells:

- **#DIV/0!** A divide-by-zero error, which occurs when you create a formula with a divisor that refers to a blank cell.

- **#NAME?** An invalid or nonexistent name. Excel also displays this error value when you fail to wrap a text string in quotation marks when you use it in a formula.

- **#VALUE** A reference to a text value in a mathematical formula.

- **#REF!** A formula reference to a deleted cell or range.

- **#N/A** A function or formula can't find a value it needs (number not available).

- **#NUM!** Invalid numeric value in a formula or a function.

- **#NULL!** A formula includes a space between two ranges to indicate an intersection, but the ranges have no cells in common.

Specific types of formula errors are checked by default. When Excel detects a formula that is inconsistent with adjacent formulas, a small triangle appears in the cell's upper-left corner. You might also see this indicator when Excel detects that a formula is incomplete, contains a faulty reference, uses unacceptable syntax, or is otherwise incorrect. When you point to the arrow, Excel displays a menu that offers options, including ignoring the error.

> **Tip** If you don't want Excel to check for certain types of errors as you work, you can change the options on the Formulas page of the Excel Options dialog box to turn off error checking altogether or to turn off specific error-checking rules.

To check for stealthier errors, use the Formula Auditing group on the Formulas tab. The Error Checking command lets you take one of several steps in response. If the selected formula has more than one calculation step, which is to say, includes more than one operator, the Show Calculation Steps button appears. Clicking it opens the Evaluate Formula dialog box, which is equivalent to clicking Evaluate Formula on the Formulas tab. Use this dialog box to follow each step in the calculations executed by the formula in the selected cell. Each time you click the Evaluate button, Excel executes the next calculation, until the final result is displayed in the dialog box.

➤ **To check for errors manually**

→ On the **Formulas** tab, click **Error Checking**.

➤ **To trace an error**

1. Select the cell that displays an error value.

2. On the **Formulas** tab, in the **Formula Auditing** group, click the **Error Checking** arrow, and then click **Trace Error**.

➤ **To turn on or off error checking options**

1. In the **Backstage view**, click **Options**.

2. In the **Excel Options** dialog box, display the **Formulas** page.

3. Under **Error Checking Rules**, clear or select the check boxes for the rules you want to use, and then click **OK**.

Troubleshooting by using tracing

The Trace Error command helps you identify the cell causing an error in a formula. When an error value is visible, click the Error Checking arrow to display the menu in the Formula Auditing group, and then click Trace Error. Excel displays arrows pointing to the cells involved in the formula.

	A	B	C	D	E	F	G	H	I
1	**Loan Calculator**								
2									
4									
5			Enter Values				Loan Summary		
6		Loan Amount	$	10,000.00		Scheduled Payment	$	188.71	
7		Annual Interest Rate	5.00 %			Scheduled Number of Payments	60		
8		Loan Period in Years	5			Actual Number of Payments	#N/A		
9		Number of Payments Per Year	12			Total Early Payments	#VALUE!		
10		Start Date of Loan	1/1/2013			Total Interest	$	41.67	
11		Optional Extra Payments	200-						
12									
13		Lender Name:							
14									
16	Pmt No.	Payment Date	Beginning Balance	Scheduled Payment	Extra Payment	Total Payment	Principal	Interest	Ending Balance
18	1	2/1/2013	$ 10,000.00	$ 188.71	#VALUE!	#VALUE!	#VALUE!	$ 41.67	#VALUE!
19	2	3/1/2013	#VALUE!	188.71	#VALUE!	#VALUE!	#VALUE!	#VALUE!	#VALUE!
20	3	4/1/2013	#VALUE!	188.71	#VALUE!	#VALUE!	#VALUE!	#VALUE!	#VALUE!
21	4	5/1/2013	#VALUE!	188.71	#VALUE!	#VALUE!	#VALUE!	#VALUE!	#VALUE!
22	5	6/1/2013	#VALUE!	188.71	#VALUE!	#VALUE!	#VALUE!	#VALUE!	#VALUE!
23	6	7/1/2013	#VALUE!	188.71	#VALUE!	#VALUE!	#VALUE!	#VALUE!	#VALUE!
24	7	8/1/2013	#VALUE!	188.71	#VALUE!	#VALUE!	#VALUE!	#VALUE!	#VALUE!
25	8	9/1/2013	#VALUE!	188.71	#VALUE!	#VALUE!	#VALUE!	#VALUE!	#VALUE!
26	9	10/1/2013	#VALUE!	188.71	#VALUE!	#VALUE!	#VALUE!	#VALUE!	#VALUE!

Amortization Table   ⊕

Beyond the obvious error values displayed in cells, you might have errors in calculations that produce questionable results. You can use the Trace Precedents and Trace Dependents commands to help audit your formulas. Precedents are cells that provide values to a formula, and dependents are cells containing the formulas that use those values. For example, if cell C3 includes the formula =A3 + B3, cells A3 and B3 are precedent cells for the formula in cell C3, and the formula in cell C3 is dependent on the values in cells A3 and B3.

> **Tip** Click Show Formulas in the Formula Auditing group to switch between viewing the formulas underlying a worksheet and the worksheet's values.

The Trace Precedents and Trace Dependents commands display blue arrows on the worksheet, pointing to related cells. Clicking once shows direct precedents or dependents; additional clicking shows each additional level of precedence or dependence. Eventually, all the other cells whose values or calculations are involved will be indicated by arrows.

You can use the arrows to navigate. Double-click any arrow to jump to the (precedent or dependent) cell on the other end of the arrow. You can use this technique to follow the trail of cell relationships.

> **Tip** You can also use the Go To Special dialog box to find precedents and dependents for a cell.

Tracing formulas in separate worksheets

You can trace precedent and dependent cells for a formula that refers to cells in a separate worksheet or workbook. When you click the command to trace the cells you want to see, Excel displays a worksheet icon to indicate that the cells are in a different worksheet. Double-click the dotted line leading from the icon to open the Go To dialog box, which contains the address of the referenced cell. Select it and click OK to activate the workbook containing the formula.

➤ **To track precedent cells**

1. Select a cell containing a formula.

2. On the **Formulas** tab, in the **Formula Auditing** group, click **Trace Precedents**.

3. Click **Trace Precedents** again to see the next layer of relationships.

➤ **To track dependent cells**

1. Select a cell containing a formula.

2. On the **Formulas** tab, in the **Formula Auditing** group, click **Trace Dependents**.

3. Click **Trace Dependents** again to see the next layer of relationships.

➤ **To remove the formula auditing arrows**

1. On the **Formula** tab, in the **Formula Auditing** group, click the arrow beside **Remove Arrows**.

2. On the menu, click **Remove Arrows** to remove all arrows, or click **Remove Precedent Arrows** or **Remove Dependent Arrows**.

Practice tasks

The practice files for these tasks are located in the MOSExcel2013Expert\Objective1 practice file folder. Save the results of the tasks in the same folder.

- Open the *ExcelExpert_1-3a*, *ExcelExpert_1-3b*, and *ExcelExpert_1-3c* workbooks, and try the following tasks:
  - ○ Review comments and accept changes in all three workbooks.
  - ○ Save each file in shared mode.
  - ○ Open the *ExcelExpert_1-3d* workbook and merge the worksheets in the three open workbooks into it.
- Open the *ExcelExpert_1-3e* workbook, select a cell in the Loan Summary area, and use the Trace Precedent and Trace Dependent commands to track the cells that affect the formulas.

Objective review

Before finishing this chapter, ensure that you have mastered the following skills:

1.1 Manage multiple workbooks
1.2 Prepare workbooks for review
1.3 Manage workbook changes

2 Apply custom formats and layouts

The skills tested in this section of the Microsoft Office Specialist Expert exams for Microsoft Excel 2013 relate to manipulating formatting and layout options. Specifically, the following objectives are associated with this set of skills:

2.1 Apply custom data formats

2.2 Apply advanced conditional formatting and filtering

2.3 Apply custom styles and templates

2.4 Prepare workbooks for internationalization and accessibility

Being a numbers program, Excel provides extensive number-format customization, beyond the extensive complement of built-in formats. You can use conditional formatting to flag critical values, and you can use custom cell styles and themes to store your custom formats.

This chapter guides you in studying methods of applying custom data formats, advanced conditional formatting and filtering, and custom styles and templates. It also describes how to work with international and accessibility requirements.

> **Practice Files** To complete the practice tasks in this chapter, you need the practice files contained in the MOSExcel2013Expert\Objective2 practice file folder. For more information, see "Download the practice files" in this book's Introduction.

2.1 Apply custom data formats

Formatting is easy when you use the buttons and controls on the ribbon. But for special formatting tasks, Excel provides tools to create custom formats you can use to display numbers, dates, and currency in specific ways not available from the ribbon.

Creating custom formats (number, time, date)

Taking control of numeric formatting begins on the Number page of the Format Cells dialog box (click the Number dialog box launcher on the Home tab, or press Ctrl+1). In the Custom category, the Type list displays the underlying codes that define all the built-in number, date, and time formats available, in addition to any custom formats you create, which are added to the bottom of the list. Many of the codes visible in this list correspond to number formats applied by clicking buttons on the ribbon. For example, clicking Fraction on the Number Format menu in the Number group on the Home tab applies the following code to selected cells:

?/?

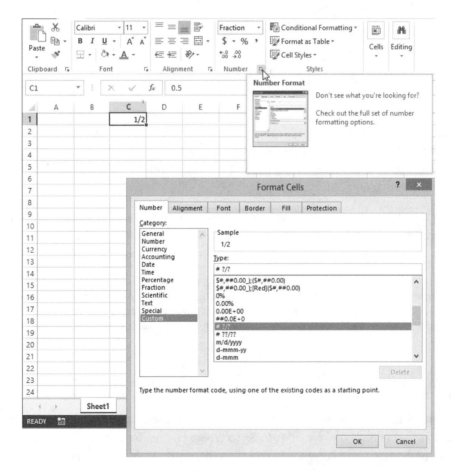

This simple code tells Excel to display the whole number value (#) in the selected cell, followed by a fraction (?/?) with single-digit values for both numerator and denominator. This effectively applies a one-digit "rounding" factor, assuming the fraction would be more precise if more placeholders were specified. For example, applying the format code # ?/? to a cell containing the value 3.45 results in the displayed value 3 4/9. The next code in the custom format code list (# ??/??) displays fractions with up to two digits of precision. If you apply this code to the same cell, the displayed value changes to 3 9/20.

The custom number format codes used by Excel are listed in the following table.

Code	Description
0	Digit placeholder. This symbol specifies the number of digits to appear on each side of the decimal point. For example, the format 0.000 displays the value .789 as 0.789. The format 0.0000 displays the value .789 as 0.7890. If a number has more digits to the right of the decimal point than the number of zeros in the format, the number displayed in the cell is rounded. For example, the format 0.00 displays the value .987 as 0.99; if the format is 0.0, .987 is rounded to 1.0.
?	Digit placeholder. Following similar rules as the 0 placeholder, except that the ? placeholder does not add insignificant zeros on either side of the decimal point. For example, applying the code 0.?? to the values 1.4 and 1.45 would display them as: 1.4 and 1.45.
#	Digit placeholder. Similar to the 0 placeholder, except that extra zeros do not appear if the number has fewer digits on either side of the decimal point than specified in the format. This symbol shows Excel where to display commas or other separating symbols. The format #,###, for example, tells Excel to display a comma after every third digit to the left of the decimal point.
.	Decimal point. This symbol determines how many digits (0 or #) appear to the right and left of the decimal point. If the format contains only # placeholders to the left of this symbol, Excel begins numbers less than 1 with a decimal point. To avoid this, use 0 as the first digit placeholder to the left of the decimal point instead of #. If you want Excel to include commas and display at least one digit to the left of the decimal point in all cases, specify the format #,##0.
%	Percentage indicator. This symbol multiplies the entry by 100 and inserts the % character.

Code	Description
/	Fraction format character. This symbol displays the fractional part of a number in a nondecimal format. The number of digit placeholders that surround this character determines the accuracy of the display. For example, the decimal fraction 0.269 when formatted with # ?/? is displayed as 1/4, but when formatted with # ???/???, it is displayed as 46/171.
,	Thousands separator. If the format contains a comma surrounded by #, 0, or ? placeholders, Excel uses commas to separate hundreds from thousands, thousands from millions, and so on. In addition, the comma acts as a rounding and scaling agent. Use one comma at the end of a format to tell Excel to round a number and display it in thousands; use two commas to tell Excel to round to the nearest million. For example, the format code #,###,###, would round 4567890 to 4,568, whereas the format code #,###,###,, would round it to 5.
E– E+ e– e+	Scientific format characters. If a format contains one 0 or # to the right of an E–, E+, e–, or e+, Excel displays the number in scientific notation and inserts E or e in the displayed value. The number of 0 or # placeholders to the right of the E or e determines the minimum number of digits in the exponent. Use E– or e– to place a negative sign by negative exponents; use E+ or e+ to place a negative sign by negative exponents and a positive sign by positive exponents.
$ – + / ( ) space	Standard formatting characters. Typing any of these symbols adds the actual corresponding character directly to your format.
\	Literal demarcation character. Precede each character you want to display in the cell—except for : $ – + / ( ) and space—with a backslash. (Excel does not display the backslash.) For example, the format code #,##0 \D;–#,##0 \C displays positive numbers followed by a space and a D and displays negative numbers followed by a space and a C. To insert several characters, use the quotation-mark technique described later in this table in the "Text" table entry.
_	Underscore. This code leaves space equal to the width of the next character. For example, _) leaves a space equal to the width of the close parenthesis. Use this formatting character for alignment purposes.
"Text"	Literal character string. This format code works like the backslash technique except that all text can be included within one set of double quotation marks without using a separate demarcation character for each literal character.
*	Repetition initiator. This code repeats the next character in the format enough times to fill the column width. Use only one asterisk in the format.
@	Text placeholder. If the cell contains text, this placeholder inserts that text in the format where the @ appears. For example, the format code "This is a" @ displays This is a debit in a cell containing the word debit.

If you study the list of custom format codes in the Format Cells dialog box, you can begin to understand how the elements work together. Select a cell containing a number and apply any format by using buttons on the ribbon. Then open the Format Cells dialog box to determine what the custom format code looks like.

Here is the underlying code behind the format applied by clicking the Accounting Number Format button ($) on the Home tab:

_($* #,##0.00_);_($* (#,##0.00);_($* "-"??_);_(@_)

Format codes can have up to four sections, separated by semicolons, as shown in the preceding example.

_($* #,##0.00_)	The first section defines the format for positive numbers.
_($* (#,##0.00)	The second section defines the format for negative numbers.
_($* "-"??_)	The third section defines the format for zero values.
_(@_)	The fourth section defines the format for text.

Notice that each section of the format code begins with an underscore. Referring to the format code definitions listed earlier, the underscore is a character that is used to create a space equal to the width of the next character, which in this case (and in most cases) is a parenthesis. (Using parentheses to surround negative values is standard accounting practice.) The underscore is used to arrange numbers in a column so that the decimal points line up, even when a number is negative. The underscore at the end of the first format code adds a parenthesis-sized space after positive numbers, to compensate for the parentheses that appear at the end of negative numbers. There are even spaces added in the fourth code section, so that text also lines up properly. If you substituted a different character after the underscore, the size of the inserted space would change accordingly.

The asterisk character repeats the next character as many times as necessary to fill the space available in the cell. In this case, the next character is a space. The result is that, as in all Accounting formats, the dollar sign is forced to appear on the left in a cell, while the number remains right-justified.

Creating custom accounting formats

You can create your own formats, but usually it's easier to modify existing code that comes close to what you're looking for. For example, suppose you want to use an accounting format, but you'd like to handle text differently. Start by applying the Accounting number format to a cell. Then on the Number page of the Format Cells dialog box, click the Custom category.

The @ symbol in the last section of a format code (after the last semicolon) instructs Excel to display any text in the cell. For example, try replacing the @ symbol with the words "Text Entry" (including the quotation marks). Instead of displaying the actual text contents of a cell, any cell formatted by using this custom code displays *Text Entry* if the cell contains any text, even a space character.

When you modify an existing format code, the old code remains unchanged. You cannot delete or overwrite built-in formats.

➤ **To create a custom Accounting format**

1. Select a cell containing a number.

2. On the **Home** tab, in the **Number** group, click the **Accounting Number Format** button, and then press **Ctrl+1**.

3. In the **Format Cells** dialog box, on the **Number** page, click the **Custom** category.

4. In the **Type** box, edit the code as needed, and then click **OK**.

➤ **To delete a custom format**

1. Press **Ctrl+1**.

2. In the **Format Cells** dialog box, on the **Number** page, click the **Custom** category.

3. Select the custom format code you want to delete.

4. Press the **Delete** button below the **Type** list, and then click **OK**.

Creating custom date formats

November 12, 2013 is the 41,590th day since (and including) January 1, 1900. If you enter 11/12/2013 into a cell and then apply the General format, the actual value—or the *date value*—is displayed as 41590. This is how Excel calculates the passage of time. (Hours, minutes, and seconds are represented as decimals.)

When you enter a date "in format" (for example, entering *11/12/2013* into an unformatted cell), Excel applies the appropriate built-in format, if there is one that corresponds. Because date formatting can be tricky, Excel provides built-in formats for most of the commonly used date formats. If you click the Date category on the Number page of the Format Cells dialog box, the Type list shows in-format examples that Excel recognizes as you type. When you complete an entry that matches an example, Excel applies the corresponding format. If you click the Custom category that has a date-formatted cell selected, the list of built-in formats is displayed, expressed as codes.

The following table lists Excel date-format codes. Strictly speaking, General is not a date-format code, but it is what you use to reveal the underlying serial date value. Interestingly, if you enter *General* as a custom code in the Type box, it actually does apply the General format.

Code	Description
General	Number in General (serial value) format
d	Day number without leading zero (1–31)
dd	Day number with leading zero (01–31)
ddd	Day-of-week abbreviation (Sun–Sat)
dddd	Complete day-of-week name (Sunday–Saturday)
m	Month number without leading zero (1–12)
mm	Month number with leading zero (01–12)
mmm	Month name abbreviation (Jan–Dec)
mmmm	Complete month name (January–December)
yy	Last two digits of year number (00–99)
yyyy	Complete four-digit year number (1900–2078)

You can combine these codes in almost any way. For example, if the Long Date format offered on the Number Format menu in the Number group on the Home tab is close but not quite what you need, start with it and modify it. Format a cell as Long Date and then press Ctrl+1 to open the Format Cells dialog box. Click the Custom category to display the underlying code:

[$-F800]dddd, mmmm dd, yyyy

Note that the bracketed portion is a special internal code that instructs Excel to adjust the format to match regional date and time settings. You can leave it there if you prefer, but for clarity, try editing the code as follows:

dddd, mmmm dd, yyyy hh:mm:ss

Notice that *d* codes appear twice in this date format. The day is displayed as a day of the week (*dddd*) and as a number (*dd*).

> **Tip** Format codes preceded by bracketed regional codes like *[$-F409]* are generated by Excel on the fly, according to system regional settings, and you can delete them, unlike other built-in codes. Excel will recreate them if necessary.

After you add a custom date or time format to the Type list, you can apply it to any date or time entry. Select the Custom category, select the format in the Type list, and then click OK to apply the format.

➤ **To create a custom Date format**

1. Select the cell or cells you want to format, and then press **Ctrl+1**.

2. In the **Format Cells** dialog box, on the **Number** page, click the **Date** category.

3. Select the date format that most resembles the one you want to create.

4. Click the **Custom** category.

5. In the edit box at the top of the **Type** list, edit the code as needed, and then click **OK**.

Creating custom time formats

At 11:12 AM, exactly 46.667 percent of the day is over. If you enter *.46667* into a cell and then apply the Time format, the value is displayed as 11:12:00 AM.

Like date formats, when you enter a time "in format" (11:12 AM) into an unformatted cell, Excel applies the appropriate built-in format, if there is one that corresponds. If you click the Custom category on the Number page of the Format Cells dialog box when a time-formatted cell is selected, the Type list shows all the in-format examples that Excel recognizes. The codes used in these examples are listed in the following table.

Code	Description
General	Number in General (serial value) format
h	Hour without leading zero (0–23)
hh	Hour with leading zero (00–23)
m	Minute without leading zero (0–59)
mm	Minute with leading zero (00–59)
s	Second without leading zero (0–59)
ss	Second with leading zero (00–59)
s.0	Second and tenths of a second without leading zero
s.00	Second without leading zero; hundredths of a second with leading zero
ss.0	Second with leading zero; tenths of a second without leading zero
ss.00	Second and hundredths of a second with leading zero
AM/PM	Time in AM/PM notation
am/pm	Time in am/pm notation
A/P	Time in A/P notation
a/p	Time in a/p notation

In time formats, leading zeros are often used when military-style time is preferred. For example, the Time format available on the Number Format menu in the Number group on the Home tab displays time in AM/PM style, with seconds displayed. Press Ctrl+1, and then click the Custom category on the Number page of the Format Cells dialog box to display the underlying code:

[$-F400]hh:mm:ss AM/PM

The bracketed portion is a special internal code that instructs Excel to adjust the time format to match regional date and time settings.

After applying the Time format, a cell containing the value 0.59886 displays the time 2:22:22 PM. If you press Ctrl+1 again and click the Custom category, you can delete the bracketed portion of the format code, and "AM/PM," which changes the format to use a 24-hour clock:

hh:mm:ss

The resulting time is displayed as 14:22:22. Even though you just "created" the hh:mm:ss format, it is actually the same as a built-in format, so you can't delete it.

> **Tip** Date and time codes with brackets [ ] around the first code section display elapsed time, not time of day. Brackets can be placed around the first section only.

➤ **To create a custom Time format**

1. Select the cell or cells you want to format, and then press **Ctrl+1**.

2. In the **Format Cells** dialog box, on the **Number** page, click the **Time** category.

3. Select the time format that most resembles the one you want to create.

4. Click the **Custom** category.

5. In the **Type** box, edit the code as needed, and then click **OK**.

Using advanced Fill Series options

You can use the fill handle or the Auto Fill Options menu to quickly extend a series of numbers, dates, days, weeks, months, and even text entries with trailing numbers. For more options, you can use the options in the Series dialog box to create linear or growth series, specify incremental step values, and indicate a value at which to stop extending the series. To open the Series dialog box, click the Fill arrow in the Editing group on the Home tab, and then click Series.

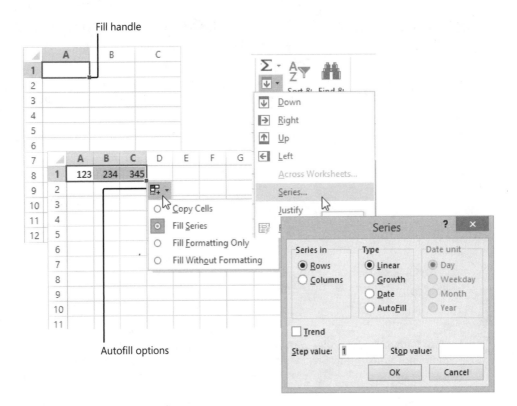

Linear series are created by *adding* the step value to the starting value and each subsequent value; the increment between values in the series remains the same. Growth
series are created by *multiplying* the starting value and each subsequent value by the
step value; the increment between values in the series increases. If you select Date as the
series type, the Date Unit options are activated, which you can use to select a calendar
increment of days, weekdays only, months, or years.

For example, if you select a range of 10 cells beginning with three cells containing the
values 123, 234, and 345, and then open the Series dialog box, Excel displays the calculated Step Value, 111, and Linear is selected. If you click OK to accept the defaults (the
same as if you had dragged the fill handle), Excel performs a linear series fill. If you select
the same three values alone, and then drag the fill handle using the mouse button on the
right, a menu appears, offering other options, including Growth Trend, which is equivalent to clicking Growth in the Series dialog box.

> **Tip** A linear series creates a straight line on a chart; a growth series creates a curve.

The AutoFill capabilities of Excel go beyond extrapolating trends, and can also extend simple nonnumeric series including days of the week, months, and even text that has trailing digits such as Product 1, simply by dragging the fill handle.

Creating custom fill sequences

AutoFill uses built-in lists to extend frequently used sequences that are in neither numerical nor alphabetical order, such as days of the week and months. When you drag the fill handle of a cell containing any item in that list, AutoFill extends the sequence, and repeats it as necessary.

To create a custom fill sequence, first enter your list into a cell range somewhere in the workbook. You can keep it on a separate worksheet if you like, but you can also simply delete the cell entries after defining the custom fill sequence. Select it and add it to the Custom Lists dialog box, accessible via the Advanced page of the Excel Options dialog box. You can import as many custom lists as needed.

> **Tip** As you drag the fill handle to extend a series, Excel displays a ScreenTip near the cursor, showing the extended value at each cell along the way.

➤ To create a custom fill sequence

1. Enter your custom list into an empty cell range, and then select the range.

2. In the **Backstage** view (accessed by clicking the **File** tab), click **Options**.

3. On the **Advanced** page of the **Excel Options** dialog box, in the **General** section, click the **Edit Custom Lists** button.

4. In the **Custom Lists** dialog box, with your selected cells displayed in the **Import list from cells** box, click the **Import** button, and then click **OK**.

Practice tasks

The practice file for these tasks is located in the MOSExcel2013Expert\Objective2 practice file folder. Save the results of the tasks in the same folder.

- Open the *ExcelExpert_2-1* workbook, and then try the following tasks:
  - ○ Modify one of the built-in accounting formats to display a text message when the cell's displayed value equals zero.
  - ○ Create a custom date format that begins with the year.
  - ○ Enter a random sequence of numbers and extend a growth series.
  - ○ Create a custom fill sequence that uses the names of five people you know, sorted by height, shortest to tallest.

2.2 Apply advanced conditional formatting and filtering

Conditional formatting is typically applied to a range of cells and responds differently depending on the contents of each cell. You can use conditional formatting to flag discrepancies, indicate relative values, highlight specific or duplicate values, and more. The Conditional Formatting menu contains five categories of prepackaged rules you can choose from, which are described in the following list.

- **Highlight Cells Rules** This category of rules uses comparison operators to determine which cells to highlight, including greater than, less than, equal to, and between. You can also use Highlight Cells Rules to highlight duplicate values or dates within a specified range.

	D	E	F	G
	Division	Sales	Units	Unit Price
	United States	1,019.32	34	29.98
	United States	1,693.86	37	45.78
	Asia	10,724.34	33	324.98
	Canada	34,695.70	130	266.89
	Asia	1,049.30	35	29.98
	United States	47.00	10	4.70
	Europe	14,769.28	47	314.24
	United States	2,810.60	20	140.53

Greater Than ? ✕

Format cells that are GREATER THAN:

20,000 ▦ with Light Red Fill with Dark Red Text ▾

OK Cancel

- **Top/Bottom Rules** You can use this category of rules to highlight figures on the top or bottom of the value scale, using numbers, percentages, or averages. The default for both "top" commands is 10, but you can use any number (for example, top 500) or any percentage.

	D	E	F	G
	Division	Sales	Units	Unit Price
	United States	1,019.32	34	29.98
	United States	1,693.86	37	45.78
	Asia	10,724.34	33	324.98
	Canada	34,695.70	130	266.89
	Asia	1,049.30	35	29.98
	United States	47.00	10	4.70
	Europe	14,769.28	47	314.24
	United States	2,810.60	20	140.53

Bottom 10% ? ✕

Format cells that rank in the BOTTOM:

25 ↕ % with Light Red Fill with Dark Red Text ▾

OK Cancel

- **Data Bars** These create a "bar chart" style display on the worksheet, where the relative value in each cell in the range is displayed as a bar of color; the greater the value, the longer the bar. The bars are sized relative to the sum of all values specified in the conditionally formatted range.

- **Color Scales** These are sets of colors that denote relative values, and can help visualize the distribution of values across a worksheet.

- **Icon Sets** You can use these to indicate relative values by using sets of 3, 4, or 5 icons, each representing a range of values. Icons are inserted inside the cell, which usually requires widening the column to accommodate them.

In the dialog boxes for both Highlight Cells and Top/Bottom rules, you can modify the default formats by selecting a different option in the With list. One of the options in that list is Custom Format, which displays the Format Cells dialog box, where you can tailor the number, font, border, and fill formatting. But you can gain far more control over conditional formatting by creating your own rules, as described in the next topic.

Creating custom conditional formats

You can build your own custom formats by clicking the New Rule command on the Conditional Formatting menu (or the More Rules command at the bottom of any sub-menu) to display the New Formatting Rule dialog box. You can also start with a built-in rule that meets most of your requirements, and then modify it. For example, start with a Highlight Cells rule, and then click the Manage Rules command to modify rule types, values, and operators, and to open the Format Cells dialog box for more options. Click the Edit Rule button in the Conditional Formatting Rules Manager dialog box to open the Edit Formatting Rule dialog box.

Each Rule Type and Style in the Edit Formatting Rule dialog box has its own set of options. For example, the first rule type—Format All Cells Based On Their Values—is the one you use to apply color scales, data bars, and icon sets. Selecting this rule type changes the Rule Description area to include a Format Style list; click Data Bar to display the Minimum and Maximum lists, where you can select values for numbers, percentages, and even percentiles.

The Negative Value And Axis button in the Edit Formatting Rule dialog box displays a settings dialog box you can use to adjust how Excel handles negative values in data bars. Within each cell, positive values are on the right and negative values are on the left of a flexible center line, whose position depends upon the weight of total values on one side or the other.

Using the options in the Edit Formatting Rule dialog box, you can customize the display of data bars to include minimums and maximums for values, percentages, or percentiles; you can change the direction of the bars; and you can change the border and fill colors.

➤ **To apply a conditional format**

1. Select the cells you want to format.

2. On the **Home** tab, in the **Styles** group, click **Conditional Formatting**.

3. Select a rule type and a sub-type (for example, Data Bars, Gradient Fill).

4. Enter the required parameters (none required for Data Bars, Color Scales, or Icon Sets), and then click **OK**.

➤ **To create a custom conditional formatting rule**

1. Select the cells you want to format.

2. Click **Conditional Formatting**, and then click **New Rule**.

3. In the **New Formatting Rule** dialog box, select a rule type.

4. In the **Edit the Rule Description** area, make formatting choices, and then click **OK**.

Using functions to format cells

The last rule type in the Edit Formatting Rule dialog box is Use A Formula To Determine Which Cells To Format. The classic example of a conditional formatting formula employs a MOD function to apply every-other-row-shading. This motif, originally designed to make data easier to read on dot-matrix tractor-feed printouts, is similar to the default formatting applied to Excel tables.

You select the entire sheet by clicking the Select All button, located at the intersection of the row and column headers. Then in the Edit Formatting Rule dialog box, click Use A Formula To Determine Which Cells To Format. In the Format Values Where This Formula Is True box, enter the following formula:

=MOD(ROW(),2)=1

Then click the Format button, and in the Format Cells dialog box, select the formatting options you want to use.

> **Tip** With any conditional formatting rule you create, don't forget to specify a distinctive format. If you're testing a rule and you think it should work, but nothing seems to happen, make sure you specified a format that will be easily visible. Simply changing the font, for example, might not suffice.

➤ **To create a conditional formatting rule by using a function**

1. Select the cells you want to format.

2. On the **Home** tab, in the **Styles** group, click **Conditional Formatting**, and then click **New Rule**.

3. Select the **Use a formula to determine which cells to format** rule type.

4. Enter a formula in the edit box (remember to include an = sign).

5. Click the **Format** button, and select options in the **Format Cells** dialog box.

6. Click **OK** in the **Format Cells** dialog box, and again in the **New Formatting Rule** dialog box.

Creating advanced filters

You can apply more than one conditional format to the same cells. For example, you can use a Top 10 rule to identify sales leaders, a Bottom 10 rule to identify sales challenges, and a Highlight Cells rule to highlight blank cells, which might indicate other problems.

You can also apply conditional formats to PivotTables. Because PivotTables are dynamic, the number of rows and columns displayed in them, in addition to the data itself, can change drastically when you make changes to the table. You can apply rules to selected cells as usual, but with PivotTables, you have the option of applying rules to the structure—the hierarchy—of the PivotTable itself, allowing the formatting to more accurately respond to changes made to the PivotTable. When you click the Conditional Formatting menu, and then click New Rule when the active cell is within the values area of a PivotTable, three new options appear at the top of the New Formatting Rule dialog box (or the Edit Formatting Rule dialog box, if you clicked Edit Rule in the Conditional Formatting Rules Manager.) The three options are as follows:

- **Selected Cells** This is the default option. The current reference is visible at the top of the dialog box. Use this option if you want to apply the rule to only part of a table, including noncontiguous cells. First, select the cells to format before opening the dialog box so that the cell references are inserted for you. This is called *scoping by selection*.

- **All Cells Showing * Values** (* varies depending on your field names) This applies the rule to all levels (hierarchies) in the values field of the PivotTable, including totals and subtotals. There is no need to select cells. This is called *scoping by value field*.

- **All Cells Showing * Values for * and *** This applies the rule to only one level in the hierarchy; totals and subtotals are excluded. There is no need to select cells. This is called *scoping by corresponding field*.

For example, you could apply three conditional formatting rules to a PivotTable report: A Highlight Cells rule could flag blank cells by using the second (value field) option, just in case there are any blank totals. Top 10% and Bottom 10% rules employ the third (corresponding field) option so that totals and subtotals are excluded.

Sum of Sales	Asia	Canada	Europe	South America	United States	Grand Total
0	130,906	147,961	99,051	115,612	140,644	634,174
1	4,229	4,484	37,488	1,023	2,855	50,079
2			14,734	40		
3	71,445	62,103	176			
4	116,380	92,617	102			
5	49,984	46,241	20			
6	40,696	90,209	29			
7	30,285	6,296	52			
8	60,575	63,484	90			
Grand Total	504,500	528,129	649			

Conditional Formatting Rules Manager

Show formatting rules for: Current Selection

New Rule... | Edit Rule... | Delete Rule

Rule (applied in order shown)	Format	Applies to	Stop If True
Cell contains a blank val...	AaBbCcYyZz	Sum of Sales	☑
Top 10 - All Values	AaBbCcYyZz	Sum of Sales, Team | Division	☐
Bottom 10% - All Values	AaBbCcYyZz	Sum of Sales, Team | Division	☐

OK | Cancel | Apply

Managing conditional formatting rules

Experimenting with conditional formatting tends to cause the accumulation of rules, but you might not notice, because when you click Manage Rules on the Conditional Formatting menu, the Conditional Formatting Rules Manager dialog box displays only rules that apply to the currently selected cells. The default option selected in the Show Formatting Rules For list is Current Selection, but the list includes options for the entire sheet, any other sheets in the workbook, and any PivotTables that might exist in the workbook. You can click the Add Rule button if you decide to add a rule while perusing available rules. To edit a rule, select one and click Edit Rule or Delete Rule.

If you apply a format to a selected PivotTable cell or range when you meant to apply it to the table hierarchy, immediately click the icon that appears adjacent to the cell to display the shortcut menu that offers the same three options as the Conditional Formatting Rules Manager dialog box.

⊿	A	B	C	D	E	F	G	H	I
1	Sum of Sales	Division ▾							
2	Team ▾	Asia	Canada	Europe	South America	United States	Grand Total		
3	0	130,906	🔲 ▾ 961	99,051	115,612	140,644	634,174		
4	1	4,229							
5	2								
6	3	71,445							
7	4	116,380							
8	5	49,984							
9	6	40,696	90,209	29,754	39,569	59,168	259,397		
10	7	30,285	6,296	52,235	5,461	18,864	113,141		
11	8	60,575	63,484	90,484	84,279	49,829	348,651		
12	Grand Total	504,500	528,129	649,429	561,838	433,686	2,677,583		
13									

Apply formatting rule to ...

⊙ Selected cells

○ All cells showing "Sum of Sales" values

○ All cells showing "Sum of Sales" values for "Team" and "Division"

➤ **To edit a conditional formatting rule**

1. On the **Home** tab, in the **Styles** group, click **Conditional Formatting**, and then click **Manage Rules**.

2. In the **Conditional Formatting Rules Manager** dialog box, select the rule you want to edit, and then click the **Edit Rule** button.

3. Make changes in the **Edit Formatting Rule** dialog box. (If necessary, click the **Format** button to open the **Format Cells** dialog box for more options.)

4. Click **OK** as needed to close any open dialog boxes.

➤ **To manage conditional formatting rules**

1. On the **Home** tab, in the **Styles** group, click **Conditional Formatting**, and then click **Manage Rules**.

2. Select a rule, and do one or more of the following:

   ⊠ Delete it by clicking the **Delete Rule** button.

   ⊠ Change the order it is applied in by clicking the **Move Up** or **Move Down** arrows next to the **Delete Rule** button.

   ⊠ Edit a rule by clicking the **Edit Rule** button.

   ⊠ Add a new rule by clicking the **New Rule** button.

➤ **To clear all conditional formatting rules**

1. In the **Styles** group, click **Conditional Formatting**, and then click **Clear Rules**.

2. On the **Clear Rules** menu, click **Clear Rules from Selected Cells**, **Clear Rules from Entire Sheet**, **Clear Rules from This Table**, or **Clear Rules from This PivotTable**.

Practice tasks

The practice file for these tasks is located in the MOSExcel2013Expert\Objective2 practice file folder. Save the results of the tasks in the same folder.

- Open the *ExcelExpert_2-2* workbook, and then try the following tasks:
  - On the Over20K worksheet, apply an additional Highlight Cells conditional format in column E, and then modify it.
  - On the Formulas worksheet, edit the rule to change the formatting.
  - On the Pivot worksheet, change the displayed data by selecting different teams or divisions. Change one of the rules.

2.3 Apply custom styles and templates

By using a template, you can create new workbooks that have predetermined column and row headings, formulas, formatting, and other elements already in place. For example, organizations might build a budget from the bottom up by distributing workbooks to product managers who complete and forward the workbooks to group managers, who summarize the data and send a report to the vice president. In a process like this, using a workbook with a common structure supplied by a template greatly facilitates the consolidation, summary, and analysis of data.

Creating custom templates

The first step in designing a template is to set up a workbook with the formulas, formatting, and other elements you need. In a budget template, you might include worksheets for each month or each fiscal quarter and rows or columns that match budget categories.

> **Tip** To help prevent changes to a workbook template, you can assign a password to the template. You can assign one password to access the workbook, and assign a different password in order to modify the workbook. For more information, see the "Protecting workbooks for sharing" topic of section 1.2, "Prepare workbooks for review."

In the Backstage view, click Save if the workbook has not been saved, or click Save As if it has been saved, and select Excel Template (.xltx) from the Save as Type list. As soon as you do so, Excel switches the active folder to the specified templates folder. By default,

Excel 2013 stores templates under a user's profile in the folder C:\Users*user name*\ Documents\Custom Office Templates (in previous editions of Office, C:\Users*user name*\ AppData\Roaming\Microsoft\Templates).

> **Tip** To change the default folder where your templates are stored, in the Backstage view, click Options, and then click Save. Enter the location of the folder in the Default Personal Templates Location box.

When you first save a template in the specified template location, Excel adds a Personal template category on the New page of the Backstage view. Excel presents a generic thumbnail image of each template you save here, which you can click to open a new copy.

> **Strategy** The objective domain for Microsoft Office Specialist Exam 77-428, "MOS Excel 2013 Expert, Part 2" includes "Creating and modifying custom templates" under Objective 2.3. This section discusses modifying formatting, including cell styles, color and font formats, and themes, which together comprise a discussion of how to modify a template, or any other worksheet. For more information about opening and saving templates and managing styles, see section 1.1, "Manage multiple workbooks."

➤ To save a workbook as a template by using a password

1. In the **Backstage** view, click **Save As**, select a location in the center pane, and then click the **Browse** button in the right pane.

2. In the **Save As** dialog box, in the **Save as type** list, click **Excel Template (*.xltx)**, **Excel Macro-Enabled Template (*.xltm)**, or **Excel 97-2003 Template (*.xlt)**.

3. Click **Tools**, and then click **General Options**.

4. In the **General Options** dialog box, enter a password to open the file and a separate password to control modifications.

5. Click **OK** in the **General Options** dialog box, confirm the passwords, click **OK** in the subsequent two dialog boxes, and then click **Save** in the **Save As** dialog box.

➤ To modify a custom template

1. In the **Backstage** view, click **Open**.

2. In the **Excel Options** dialog box, click **Computer**, and then click **Browse**.

3. Open the C:\Users*user name*\Documents\Custom Office Templates folder.

4. Click the template you want to modify, and then click **Open**. Provide a password or passwords, if necessary.

5. Make modifications to the workbook.

6. In the **Backstage** view, click **Save As**. Then on the **Save As** page, select a place in the center pane, and click **Browse** in the right pane.

7. In the **Save as type** list, ensure that **Excel Template (*.xltx)** is selected. If the template includes macros, select **Excel Macro-Enabled Template (*.xltm)**.

8. Click the **Save** button to close the dialog box.

> **See Also** For information about checking the compatibility of an Excel 2013 workbook with earlier versions of Excel, see section 1.2, "Prepare workbooks for review."

Creating and modifying cell styles

Cell Styles are combinations of formats—including font, fill, border, number, alignment, and/or protection formats—that can be applied with a single click of the mouse. Clicking Cell Styles on the Home tab displays a gallery of built-in styles. In addition to familiar word-processing styles like *Heading 1* and *Normal*, Excel includes worksheet-oriented styles to apply number formats and shading variations, and offers styles that can be helpful when building interactive data models.

The New Cell Style command at the bottom of the Cell Styles menu opens the Style dialog box, in which you can select the types of formats you want to apply. To choose more options, click the Format button, which opens the Format Cells dialog box.

If you select any nondefault options on any page in the Format Cells dialog box, the corresponding check box is selected when you return to the Style dialog box. If you decide to exclude any format type, clear the check box in the Style dialog box before clicking OK.

Custom Styles appear at the top of the Cell Styles menu, under the Custom heading, which does not appear unless you have defined a style. You can modify custom styles but not built-in styles.

> **See Also** For information about exporting custom cell styles, see the "Copying styles between templates" topic in section 1.1, "Manage multiple workbooks."

➤ **To create a new cell style**

1. On the **Home** tab, in the **Styles** group, click the **Cell Styles** button, and then click **New Cell Style**.

2. In the **Style** dialog box, click **Format**.

3. In the **Format Cells** dialog box, choose formatting options, and then click OK.

4. In the **Style** dialog box, clear check boxes for any format categories you do not want to include, enter a style name, and then click **OK**.

➤ **To modify a cell style**

1. On the **Home** tab, in the **Styles** group, click the **Cell Styles** button.

2. In the **Custom** category, right-click the custom style you want to modify, and then click **Modify**.

3. In the **Style** dialog box, click **Format**.

4. In the **Format Cells** dialog box, make formatting modifications, and then click **OK**.

5. In the **Style** dialog box, ensure that only the format categories that you want to include are selected, and then click **OK**.

Creating custom color and font formats

You can create custom color formats in two ways in Excel: by creating a cell style that applies font color, border color, and/or fill color to a cell or selection; or by creating a color scheme that determines the entire palette of colors used by all styles and themes. By using the latter approach when creating templates, you can establish design consistency and easily create complementary documents from Excel and other Microsoft Office programs.

> **See Also** For more information, see "Creating themes," later in this section.

Use the options in the Themes group on the Page Layout tab to apply color, font, and effects formats. Clicking the Colors button displays palettes, the first of which is the default color set for new worksheets, unless you have already created custom color sets, which always appear first in the palettes. Modify the color set by clicking Customize Colors below the palettes. If the color you need isn't available in any of the palettes in the Create New Theme Colors dialog box, click More Colors (available at the bottom of each Theme Colors palette). The Standard page of the Colors dialog box includes a wider palette of clickable colors, or you can enter precise RGB (red, green, blue) or HSL (hue, saturation, luminosity) values directly on the Custom page.

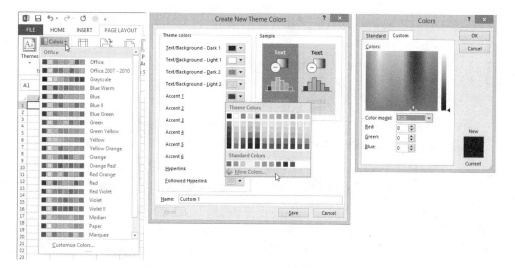

> **Tip** The six accent colors in the Create New Theme Colors dialog box correspond to accent styles in the Themed Cell Styles section of the Cell Styles gallery on the Home tab.

You can create custom font sets that control two cell styles: Heading, which controls the built-in heading styles, and Body, which determines the font used in all other cells that do not have specific formatting applied. When you create color sets or font sets, your custom sets appear at the top of the corresponding palette under the Custom category, which only appears when custom sets are available.

You cannot create custom effects sets.

> **To create a custom color set**

1. On the **Page Layout** tab, in the **Themes** group, click the **Colors** button, and then click **Customize Colors**.

2. In the **Create New Theme Colors** dialog box, select the colors you want to use for each style.

3. In the **Name** box, enter a name for the color set, and then click **Save**.

> **To create a custom font set**

1. On the **Page Layout** tab, click the **Fonts** button, and then click **Customize Fonts**.

2. In the **Create New Theme Fonts** dialog box, select the fonts you want for **Heading** and **Body**.

3. Enter a name for the font set in the Name box, and then click **Save**.

Creating themes

Themes are collections of font, color, and effects formats used to control the overall appearance of workbooks. Themes are shared across Office programs, so any Office document employing the same theme will have a similar appearance. When building templates for multiple users and multiple purposes, sharing common themes makes it easy to maintain design consistency.

You are essentially creating a "theme" whenever you work with the Colors, Fonts, and Effects buttons in the Themes group on the Page Layout tab. However, in order to use the same collection of formats with other documents, you need to save your choices and name them as a new theme.

The Save Current Theme command at the bottom of the Themes menu on the Page Layout tab saves your theme in the following location:

C:\Users*user name*\AppData\Roaming\Microsoft\Templates\Document Themes

After you save your theme, a Custom category appears at the top of the Themes menu, presenting your custom themes.

> **Tip** You can remove unwanted saved themes by right-clicking a thumbnail in the Custom category and clicking Delete.

After you save a theme, it is available when creating other workbooks and when creating documents with other Office programs. For example, after you create a theme, open a Microsoft Word document, click the Themes button on the Design tab, and in the Custom category, notice that your theme is listed there.

➤ **To create a theme**

1. On the **Page Layout** tab, in the **Themes** group, select formats by using the options on the **Colors**, **Fonts**, and **Effects** menus.

2. Click the **Themes** button, and then click the **Save Current Theme** command at the bottom of the menu.

3. In the **Save Current Theme** dialog box, give your theme a name, and then dick **OK**.

> ➤ **To edit a theme**

1. Apply the theme you want to modify to the current workbook.

2. On the **Page Layout** tab, in the **Themes** group, edit the formats by using the options on the **Colors**, **Fonts**, and **Effects** menus.

3. Click the **Themes** button, and then click the **Save Current Theme** command at the bottom of the menu.

4. Keep the same file name, and then click **Save**.

5. In the **Confirm Save As** dialog box, click **Yes**.

Creating form fields

One way you can collect and present data in Excel is through the use of form controls that you add to a worksheet. Controls such as list boxes, check boxes, and command buttons help structure a worksheet and manage its data, and they enable you and other users to work with data and objects on a worksheet in specific ways.

> **Important** You need the Developer tab displayed in order to create form fields. For information about displaying this tab, see the first procedure in the "Copying macros between workbooks" topic in section 1.1, "Mange multiple workbooks."

Inserting form controls

Excel displays two groups of controls when you click Insert in the Controls group on the Developer tab—Form Controls and ActiveX Controls. You can set up a form control such as a list box by using data on a worksheet. ActiveX controls are often handled program-matically by using Visual Basic for Applications (VBA), although you can set properties for ActiveX controls and use them without writing any code. The focus in this section is on Form Controls.

Point to the buttons on the Insert menu to display ScreenTips that identify each control. To create a control, click a button. This "loads" the cursor, and the next time you click or drag, the control is inserted. Resize it by dragging a handle; reposition it by dragging a border. Excel provides nine types of Form Controls:

> **Tip** For cleaner control sets, don't click. Draw controls by dragging while pressing the **Alt key. This constrains the cursor to the worksheet grid, enabling you to draw identically sized controls in perfect alignment, all in one operation.**

- **Command button** Runs macros. When you add one to a worksheet, the Assign Macro dialog box opens. Click Record to create a new macro, or choose an existing macro from any open workbook from the list.

- **Combo box** Offers items that you specify as a list of options. Insert the control, right-click it, click Format Control, and then in the Input Range box, drag to select a list of previously entered items.

- **Check box** Displays a non-exclusive option box to indicate yes (true) when selected. You can specify whether the check box is selected or cleared by default. You can put check boxes in a group box to present them as a single element, but they still generate discrete values and have individual linked cells. Users can select more than one check box in a group.

- **Option button** Displays an exclusive option button to indicate yes (true) when selected. Option buttons all share the same linked cell, but those contained in a group box function as a single element, enabling you to create more than one group. You can specify whether a button is selected or deselected by default. Users can select only one option button in a group.

- **Spin button** Creates a control to increase or decrease a value in a linked cell within a minimum and maximum that you define. You can also specify an increment other than the default value of 1.

- **Scroll bar** Changes the value in a linked cell, similar to the spin button. By using the Page Change value, you can specify the number of items that the list jumps when you click in the gray area of the scroll bar.

- **List box** Displays a set of items from which to choose. You can limit selection to a single item (Single); multiple adjacent items (Multi), selected by dragging or holding down the Shift key; or multiple non-adjacent items (Extend), selected by holding down the Ctrl key while clicking.

- **Group box** Organizes a set of controls—usually check boxes or option buttons—into a single element.

- **Label** Identifies or describes the function of a cell, range, or another control. You can use a label as you would a caption.

After inserting a control (other than a button, group box, or label), right-click the control and then click Format Control. You use the options in the Format Control dialog box to specify linked cells, list ranges, and other options pertinent to the control.

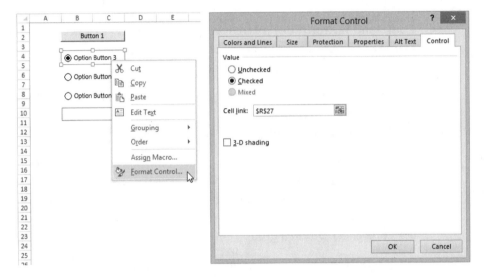

All controls, with the exception of group boxes and labels, generate values based on user selections, which you can then use in formulas, for example, or to control other aspects of the form. For each control, you need to specify a cell to receive this value by using the Cell Link box on the Control page of the Format Control dialog box. Option buttons are different, however. When you specify a linked cell for any one option button, the rest of the buttons automatically use the same cell, unless they are inside a group box, in which case only the buttons inside the box share the same linked cell. By using group boxes, you can create sets of buttons simply by drawing the box around a set of buttons, or dragging buttons inside the box. (It's a good idea to group the button and box objects so they stay together.)

For example, a group box with five option buttons returns a value of 1 if the first button is selected, 2 if the second is selected, and so on. If, instead of option buttons, you put check boxes in a group box, they generate separate values and require individual linked cells, because you can select more than one check box at a time.

Controlling the tab order of objects

If you select an object on a sheet containing several objects (including form controls) and then press the Tab key, the next object is selected. This is called the *tab order*. The order in which you create the objects—not their position on the screen—is the default tab order. Sometimes it won't matter; but working with form controls, it usually does. You want users to tab from First Name to Last Name, not from First Name to Address. And for people with low vision who rely on reader software, the order in which objects are revealed might make an even greater difference. The easiest way to keep track of this is to leave the number portion of the automatically generated labels (Button 1, Option Button 2, and so on) in the object title until the last minute. The tab order follows the original numbering, which increments for each object you create, so determine the order you want before creating controls. Unfortunately, you can't edit the tab order of most objects in Excel except form controls, and only then when used in a User Form created by using VBA. To modify the tab order of user form controls, open the VBA Editor and open the Properties window (press F4). Set the TabStop to True and the TabIndex to the desired number in the Properties Window.

➤ **To insert a button**

1. On the **Developer** tab, in the **Controls** group, click **Insert**, and then in the **Form Controls** area of the menu, click the **Button** icon.

2. Click on the worksheet where you want to place the button, and in the **Assign Macro** dialog box, type a name for the macro. Then click **Record** to record a new macro.

   Or

   In the list of macros, select the macro you want the button to run.

➤ **To insert a combo box or list box control**

1. On the **Developer** tab, on the **Insert** menu in the **Controls** group, click the **Combo Box** or **List Box** icon, and then click on the worksheet where you want to place the control.

2. Right-click the control, and then click **Format Control**.

3. On the **Control** page of the **Format Control** dialog box, specify the input range and the linked cell. For a list box, choose the selection type (**Single**, **Multi**, or **Extended**).

➤ **To insert a check box or option button control**

1. On the **Developer** tab, on the **Insert** menu in the **Controls** group, click the **Check Box** or **Option Button** icon, and then click on the worksheet where you want to place the control.

2. Right-click the control, and then click **Format Control**.

3. On the **Control** page of the **Format Control** dialog box, specify the linked cell, and whether the control should be selected or deselected by default.

➤ **To create a group of check boxes or option buttons**

1. On the **Developer** tab on the **Insert** menu in the **Controls** group, click the **Group Box** icon, click on the worksheet where you want to add the group, and then adjust the size of the box as necessary.

2. Create or drag check box or option button controls inside the group control.

➤ **To insert a spin button or scroll bar control**

1. On the **Developer** tab, on the **Insert** menu in the **Controls** group, click the **Spin Button** or **Scroll Bar** icon, and then click on the worksheet where you want to place the control.

2. Right-click the control, and then click **Format Control**.

3. On the **Control** page of the **Format Control** dialog box, specify the linked cell and any current, minimum, maximum, incremental-change, and/or page-change values.

➤ **To insert a label control**

1. On the **Developer** tab, on the **Insert** menu of the **Controls** group, click the **Label** icon, and then click on the worksheet where you want to place the control.

2. Right-click the control, and then click **Edit Text**.

3. Delete the default text, and then enter the text you want to use.

➤ **To change the default label for a command button, option button, or check box**

1. Right-click the control, and then click **Edit Text**.

2. Delete the default text, and then enter the text you want to use.

➤ **To set properties for form controls**

1. Right-click the control, and then click **Format Control**.

2. On the **Size**, **Protection**, **Properties**, and **Alt Text** pages of the **Format Control** dialog box, specify options for the control's behavior.

3. For a command button control, on the **Font**, **Alignment**, and **Margins** pages, apply additional formatting to the button and its label.

4. For check boxes and option button controls, on the **Colors and Lines** page, apply line styles and fill colors.

Practice tasks

The practice file for these tasks is located in the MOSExcel2013Expert\Objective2 practice file folder. Save the results of the tasks in the same folder.

 ⊠ Open the *ExcelExpert_2-3* workbook and then try the following tasks:

  ⊠ On the Store Inventory List worksheet, modify the theme fonts, colors, and effects, and save a new custom theme.

  ⊠ On the Form Controls worksheet, modify the combo box control and edit the input range so that two additional items appear on the list: X-Small and XXXX-Large.

  ⊠ On the Form Controls worksheet, create a new combo box that has option buttons corresponding to the options in the combo box.

2.4 Prepare workbooks for internationalization and accessibility

Whenever you share your workbooks with others, you need to make sure you're not sharing more than you intend, so removing metadata is always a good idea. If you share your workbooks with those with accessibility challenges, you have other considerations, including adding alternate text for each graphic. If your workbooks will be used by others at all, you should address both of these issues.

> **See Also** For more information about removing metadata, see the "Removing workbook metadata," in section 1. 2, "Prepare workbooks for review."

If you share your workbooks with folks from other countries, or those working in other languages or currencies, you need to ensure that you communicate the right information, in the right language, using the right symbols. This section covers some of the tools and options you can use to prepare your workbooks for any audience.

> **Strategy** The objective domain for Microsoft Office Specialist Exam 77-427, "MOS Excel 2013 Expert, Part 1" includes "Modifying tab order among workbook elements," under Objective 2.4. This is only possible in VBA, and only in special circumstances. For more information, see the sidebar, "Controlling the tab order of objects," earlier in this chapter.

Modifying worksheets for use with accessibility tools

To make it easier for anyone with a disability to read and access your data, run the Accessibility Checker to inspect your workbook and report any accessibility issues. The Accessibility Checker appears as a taskbar docked to the side of the screen.

The Inspection Results box lists issues that might make the workbook less accessible to people with functional needs. Click an item to jump to that location in the workbook.

For example, adding alternate text (alt text) describing each image, object, and control in your workbook is often critical for those with vision challenges. Alt text is invisible metadata, but reader software can't describe an object verbally if the alt text isn't there.

Here are some of the things you can do to help ensure workbook accessibility:

- Ensure that all images and objects have alternate text.
- Remove metadata (except alt text!) such as document properties.
- If you create hyperlinks, make the displayed text readable; don't display the raw URL. Always use the Text To Display box in the Hyperlink dialog box.
- Give descriptive names to all worksheets (no "Sheet1").
- Name the columns in Excel tables (no "Column1"). Specify "My Table Has Headers" when first creating the table, or select the Header Row check box on the Design tool tab and add your header information.
- Avoid using blank cells for formatting.
- Avoid merged cells.
- For audio or video, choose close-captioned versions, if available.

➤ **To inspect a workbook**

1. On the **Info** page of the **Backstage view**, click **Check for Issues**, and then click **Inspect Document**.
2. In the Excel question box stating that removed data cannot be restored, click **Yes** or **No** to saving the file.
3. In the **Document Inspector** dialog box, clear the check boxes for any content areas you don't want to inspect, and then click **Inspect**.
4. Review the inspection results that Excel displays. Click **Remove All** if you want Excel to clear up that area of the workbook for you. Otherwise, click **Close**, address the issues raised, and then run the Document Inspector again.

➤ **To check the accessibility features of a worksheet**

1. On the **Info** page of the **Backstage** view, click **Check for Issues**, and then click **Check Accessibility**.
2. In the **Accessibility Checker** pane, review the results that Excel displays. Click an entry in the list of issues, and then refer to the expanded **Additional Information** section for steps to fix the issue.
3. Run the Accessibility Checker again to verify that the issues have been resolved.

➤ **To add alt text to images, objects, or controls**

1. Right-click the graphic or object.
2. Click **Size and Properties**, and then click the **Alt Text** page in the **Format Object** (or **Format Control** or **Format Picture**) dialog box.

Displaying data in multiple international formats

In Excel, you might encounter international units of measurement, multiple languages, right-to-left languages, and even other alphabets. Excel can handle all of it, but you might need to make some accommodations when editing and proofing, especially if your workbook contains text written in more than one language.

Working in other languages

You can change the languages used for editing, interface and display, ScreenTips, and Help, and they can all be different, depending on the languages available in the edition of Windows, Excel, or Office that you are using, and the Windows language packs that you have installed. You can install additional languages from the Language page of the Excel Options dialog box.

This section focuses on what happens on a Windows 8 computer running Office Professional 2013.

The first list box shows the editing languages that are currently installed. To add another language, click the one you want from the list below the box in the Choose Editing Languages area and then click Add to insert it into the box. By using the two boxes in the Choose Display And Help Languages area, you can select separate languages for both Help and Display (interface text), if available. Just below the Display Language and Help Language boxes is an expandable View Display Languages Installed For Each Microsoft Office Program list, which is a handy way to check the language settings of your other Office programs. The Set Your ScreenTip Language list offers a more limited selection of available languages. If you click either of the two "How do I get more..." links, a page on the Office website opens in your browser, where you can download or purchase language packs, proofing tools, and ScreenTip languages.

Proofing in other languages

You might not need to switch display languages for proofing if a dictionary is available. You can change the dictionary language from the Proofing page of the Excel Options dialog box.

The Proofing page includes settings for spell-checking, a button to set AutoCorrect options, and additional menus for language modes, if any are available for the installed languages. Selecting an option in the Dictionary Language list affects the Excel spell-checker, and it also determines the default thesaurus language. Click the Thesaurus button on the Review tab to select a language from the list that appears at the bottom of the task pane.

You might already have what you need installed, depending on the language and the edition of Excel you are using. Check Control Panel for installed languages, and to download language packs, but be careful—language packs can be more than 100 megabytes.

If you add a language to the list on the Language page of the Excel Options dialog box, you might still need to enable it. The Choose Editing Languages list includes columns for Keyboard Layout and Proofing. If any language displays a Not Enabled or Not Installed link in these columns, click it to activate the Language Preferences page of Control Panel, where you can install it, or add more languages.

One more tool you can use when working in other languages is the Translate button on the Review tab, which opens a task pane. You can select the language you want to translate into, and the language to translate from, if Excel guesses incorrectly. The "to" and "from" languages are collectively referred to as *language pairs*. The Translation Options link in the task pane opens a dialog box showing the list of available language pairs that are based on dictionaries (installed and/or online), and pairs that perform machine translation via Microsoft Translator. All pairs are selected by default, but you can choose what you want.

> **Important** If your workbook contains text in multiple languages, you'll need to run a separate spell check for each language.

➤ **To proof in another language**

1. In the **Backstage** view, click **Options**.
2. On the **Proofing** page of the **Excel Options** dialog box, select the **Default Dictionary** you want.

➤ **To work in another language**

→ On the **Language** page of the **Excel Options** dialog box, select the language options you want, and then click **Set as Default**.

➤ **To check spelling in another languages**

1. On the **Proofing** page of the **Excel Options** dialog box, select the language you want in the **Dictionary Language** list, and then click **OK**.
2. On the **Review** tab, click **Spelling**, or press **F7** to start the spell check.
3. Repeat for any other languages present.

➤ **To translate selected text**

1. On the **Review** tab, click the **Translate** button.

2. In the **Research** pane, in the **Translation** area, select the languages you want in the **To** and **From** lists.

3. Select **Insert** or **Copy**.

Utilizing international symbols

For some languages, such as Latin-based languages, switching the Windows language might be unnecessary, especially if you're working mostly with numbers. You can enter most text by using your standard keyboard and insert any special international characters as you go, or you can change the keyboard layout language for more extensive foreign-language typing.

You use the Symbol dialog box to insert special characters as you type such as ö, ¿, æ, ß, and ã. You can select different fonts, each with different subsets, which generally include many variants such as Basic Latin and Cyrillic. You'll probably find the character you need in here somewhere.

Managing multiple options for body and heading fonts

The best way to work with different sets of body and/or heading fonts is to use font sets you can find or create by using the Fonts menu in the Themes group on the Page Layout tab. For example, you could use a different set of fonts for each language you work with, or create your own sets if you need to work with specific fonts not available in any of the prepackaged sets. Font sets are not limited to the worksheet or workbook, but remain available on your computer, and available to other Office programs until you delete them. Color sets created by using options on the Colors menu in the Themes group are equally persistent. Colors, themes, and effects can be saved collectively as custom themes. For more information, see the "Creating themes" topic in section 2.3, "Apply custom styles and templates."

➤ **To insert an international symbol**

   1. On the **Insert** tab, in the **Symbols** group, click the **Symbol** button.

   2. On the **Symbols** page of the **Symbol** dialog box, select the font you want in the **Font** list.

   3. Double-click a symbol to insert it.

➤ **To display the on-screen keyboard in Windows 8**

   → Click the keyboard icon in the taskbar. If the keyboard icon is not visible, right-click the taskbar, and then click **Touch Keyboard**.

Practice tasks

The practice file for these tasks is located in the MOSExcel2013Expert\Objective2 practice file folder. Save the results of the tasks in the same folder.

- Open the *ExcelExpert_2-4* workbook, and then try the following tasks:
   ○ Run the Accessibility Checker and fix the issues it finds.
   ○ On the Form Controls worksheet, add alt text to the spinner control.

Objective review

Before finishing this chapter, ensure that you have mastered the following skills:

2.1 Apply custom data formats

2.2 Apply advanced conditional formatting and filtering

2.3 Apply custom styles and templates

2.4 Prepare workbooks for internationalization and accessibility

3 Create advanced formulas

The skills tested in this section of the Microsoft Office Specialist Expert exams for Microsoft Excel 2013 relate to the creation of sophisticated formulas. Specifically, the following objectives are associated with this set of skills:

3.1 Apply functions in formulas

3.2 Look up data by using functions

3.3 Apply advanced date and time functions

3.4 Create scenarios

Most users of Excel have created formulas that include one or more of the most commonly used Excel functions, such as SUM, AVERAGE, COUNT, MAX, and MIN. However, Excel provides functions for other very specific operations.

This chapter guides you in studying methods for these other operations, such as calculating dates and times, performing statistical or financial analysis, working with text strings, and looking up values.

> **Practice Files** To complete the practice tasks in this chapter, you need the practice files contained in the MOSExcel2013Expert\Objective3 practice file folder. For more information, see "Download the practice files" in this book's Introduction.

3.1 Apply functions in formulas

Menus in the Function Library group on the Formulas tab offer functions grouped by type, including a More Functions menu. Depending on your screen size and resolution, some of the menus might include text labels, but if not, point to the menu to display a ScreenTip that has a thumbnail explanation, which might be all the information you need to proceed.

When you select a function from one of the menus, the Function Arguments dialog box opens, which you use to enter the information (called *arguments*) that the function needs to perform its calculations. The Function Arguments dialog box provides a description of the function and a description of each of the function's arguments. When you fill in the arguments, the result of the formula is displayed above the function description in the dialog box.

> **Tip** You can insert functions in Excel two additional ways. The Insert Function button (*fx*) appears both on the Formulas tab and in the formula bar. Select a category and scroll through the list of functions for a description of each one, or enter keywords in the Search For A Function box.

After a function is inserted in a cell, double-click the cell (or click in the formula bar) to edit the formula, which activates a number of helpful tools. When you click anywhere in the function in a cell or in the formula bar, a ScreenTip appears, showing you the correct syntax and displaying the currently selected argument in bold. If you click the function's name in the ScreenTip, the Help window opens, displaying a topic that describes the function. Also, the formula's dependent cells are surrounded by colored borders on the sheet; drag the borders or resize them to change the cells used as arguments.

	A	B	C	D	Sales	Units	Unit Price	H	I
AVERAGEA	▾	:	×	✓	*fx*	=AVERAGEA(E2:E1084)			
	A	B	C	D	AVERAGEA(value1, [value2], ...)	G	H		I
1	Product	Date	Team	Division	Sales	Units	Unit Price		
2	ASH-1001	1/1/2013	4	United States	1,019.32	34	29.98	=AVERAGEA(E2:E1084)	
3	ASH-1002	1/1/2013	4	United States	1,693.86	37	45.78		
4	ASH-1031	1/1/2013	4	Asia	467.94	33	14.18		
5	ASH-1032	1/1/2013	4	Canada	34,695.70	130	266.89		

Using nested functions

Functions are said to be *nested* when the parenthetical expression following the function name contains another function. A nested function performs a subordinate calculation to provide an argument for another function. For example, in the simple nested formula =INT(SUM((B2:B5)), the SUM function calculates the total first, and then the INT function rounds the result to the nearest integer.

In the formula =INT(SLN(SUM(B2:B5)),0,5), the SUM function provides an argument (cost) for the SLN function (five-year straight-line depreciation), which becomes the argument for the INT (integer) function. You can create up to 64 levels of nested functions.

Using the IF, AND, and OR functions

IF, AND, and OR are classified as logical functions in Excel. Logical operations seek a result of either TRUE or FALSE (1 or 0), and are used to test for conditions by employing the logical operators =, <, >, >=, <= or <> to create conditional tests. For example, "if A is less than B, then C; but if not, then D" describes how the IF function works. The statement "A is less than B" is a logical test, which can employ any one of the logical operators. For example, the formula =IF(B5<500, 12, 24) returns the value 12 only if cell B5 is less than 500 (TRUE); otherwise it returns the value 24. The following shows the syntax of these functions; non-italic text indicates required values.

=IF(logical_test, *value_if_true, value_if_false*)

=AND(logical1,*logical2, ...*)

=OR(logical1,*logical2, ...*)

The OR function returns TRUE if any of its arguments are true. The AND function returns TRUE only if all of its arguments are true. These two functions can be used alone, but are frequently nested within an IF function, which can also contain additional IF functions. If either of the optional arguments *value_if_true* or *value_if_false* are left blank, the IF function returns a logical value: TRUE or FALSE.

> **Strategy** The objective domain for Microsoft Office Specialist Exam 77-428 "MOS Excel Expert 2013, Part 2" includes "Utilizing the IF function in conjunction with other functions," and "Utilizing AND/OR functions" as separate topics under Objective 3.1. Both topics are covered in this section.

Using the SUMIFS, AVERAGEIFS, and COUNTIFS functions

The SUM, AVERAGE, and COUNT functions have useful "IF variants" that you can use to apply a criterion (one "if") before tallying the results: SUMIF, AVERAGEIF, and COUNTIF. Similarly, you can use the "IFS variants" to apply multiple criteria (more "ifs"): SUMIFS, AVERAGEIFS, and COUNTIFS. The following shows the syntax of these functions; non-italic arguments are required.

=SUMIF(range, criteria, *sum_range*)

=AVERAGEIF(range, criteria, *average_range*)

=COUNTIF(*range, criteria*)

=SUMIFS(sum_range, criteria_range, criteria, *criteria_range2, criteria,...*)

=AVERAGEIFS(sum_range, criteria_range, criteria, *criteria_range2, criteria,...*)

=COUNTIFS(sum_range, criteria_range, criteria, *criteria_range2, criteria,...*)

The SUMIF function adds values in the specified *sum_range* that match the criteria found in the range. For example (using named ranges instead of cell references for readability), the formula =SUMIF(Team,4,Sales) adds only those totals in the Sales column where 4 appears in the Team column.

> **Tip** If the logical operator you need is an equal sign, you can simply enter the value alone as the logical test (4). However, when using a logical operator or text (other than a defined name) in a logical test, you must always enclose the expression in double quotation marks (">4").

✓	*fx*	=SUMIF(Team,4,Sales)											∨

C	D	E	F	G	H	I	J	K	L	M	N
Team Division		**Sales**	**Units**	**Unit Price**	**US/Asia Only**	**US/Asia/$25-50**					
4	United States	1,019.32	34	29.98	$ 1,019.32	$ 1,019.32					
4	United States	1,693.86	37	45.78	$ 1,693.86	$ 1,693.86		Team 4	865,516.33		
4	Asia	467.94	33	14.18	$ 467.94	$ -		Team 4 Asia	241,522.91		
4	Canada	34,695.70	130	266.89	$ -	$ -					
4	Asia	1,049.30	35	29.98	$ 1,049.30	$ 1,049.30					
8	United States	47.00	10	4.70	$ -	$ -					

The SUMIFS function adds values in the specified *sum_range* that match the criteria applied to the range. You can add up to 127 sets of criteria.

> **Important** The *sum_range* argument is the first argument in the SUMIFS function and the last argument in the SUMIF function.

For example, the formula *=SUMIFS(Sales,Team,4,Division,"Asia")* adds only those totals in the Sales column where 4 appears in the Team column, and where Asia appears in the Division column.

The rest of the –IF and –IFS functions operate similarly.

- **COUNTIF** Counts the number of cells that match a single criterion

- **COUNTIFS** Counts the number of cells that match multiple criteria

- **AVERAGEIF** Averages the values in cells that match a single criterion

- **AVERAGEIFS** Averages the values in cells that match multiple criteria

> **Tip** When using a SUMIFS, COUNTIFS, or AVERAGIFS function, all range arguments—the *sum_range* and each *criteria_range*—must have the same number of rows and columns.

➤ **To insert a function**

1. On the **Formulas** tab, in the **Function Library** group, click the **Insert Function** button or any function category button, and then select the function you need.

2. In the **Function Arguments** dialog box, enter the arguments for the function.

➤ **To find a function**

1. On the **Formulas** tab, in the **Function Library** group, click the **Insert Function** button.

2. In the **Insert Function** dialog box, in the **Search for a function** box, enter a description of the operation you want to perform.

3. To filter the list of functions, choose a category from the **Or select a category** list.

Using financial functions

Most financial calculations are performed by using the basics: addition, subtraction, multiplication, and division. Complex financial algorithms that involve multiple steps are packaged as functions. The functions that Excel provides in its financial toolbox fall into three major subcategories: investments, depreciation, and securities.

You can find a wealth of information in the Help system about functions and how to use them; far more material than this book can cover. This section provides an overview of each subcategory and selects a few functions to examine in more detail.

> **See Also** For information about working with international currencies, see section 2.4, "Prepare workbooks for internationalization and accessibility."

Calculating investments

Investing is all about cash flow: how much, how often, for how long, and at what rate? These functions all perform similar calculations and share some of the same underlying algorithms. The investment functions in Excel include the value functions FV, PV, and NPV; the payment functions PMT, PPMT, IPMT; the rate functions RATE, IRR, and MIRR; and the periods function, NPER. The following shows the syntax of these investment functions; non-italic arguments are required.

▢ **Present value** =*PV*(rate, nper, pmt, *fv, type*)

▢ **Future value** =*FV*(rate, nper, pmt, *pv, type*)

▢ **Net present value** =*NPV*(rate, value1, *value2,...*)

▢ **Payment** =*PMT*(rate, nper, pv, *fv, type*)

▢ **Principal payment** =*PPMT*(rate, per, nper, pv, *fv, type*)

▢ **Interest payment** =*IPMT*(rate, per, nper, pv, *fv, type*)

▢ **Rate of return** =*RATE*(nper, pmt, pv, *fv, type, guess*)

- **Internal rate of return** =*IRR*(values, *guess*)

- **Modified internal rate of return** =*MIRR*(values, finance_rate, reinvest_rate)

- **Number of periods** =*NPER*(rate, pmt, pv, *fv, type*)

Arguments common to the investment functions include those in the following table.

Argument	Description
Fv	(Future value) The value of an investment at the end of the term (0 if omitted)
Value1, value2, ...	A series of payments when the amounts differ
Nper	Short for *number of periods*; the term of the investment
Pmt	Short for *payment*; a series of payments when the amounts are the same.
Type	Payment at the end of each period (0 or omitted), or the beginning (1)
Per	The period number of an individual period
Pv	Short for *present value*; the value of an investment today
Rate	Discount or interest
Guess	A starting rate (10 percent if omitted)
Finance Rate	The interest rate paid on borrowed money
Reinvest rate	The interest rate received on invested money

The payment on a loan covers both the principal (the amount of the original loan) and the interest (the cost of borrowing money). In a fixed-rate loan, the payment stays the same over the loan term, but the principal portion increases each month, whereas the interest portion decreases. The functions you can use to dissect loans are PMT, which calculates a loan payment; PPMT, which returns only the principal portion of a payment for a particular period; and IPMT, which returns the interest portion.

> **Tip** When expressing periods, you must use the same units. For example, interest is usually expressed as an annual rate, but payments are usually made on a monthly basis. For example, if the units are months and you're trying to figure out the annual interest rate, you would divide by 12 so that the units (months) match.

If you add an additional amount each month to scheduled payments, it is applied directly to the principal loan amount. This serves to reduce the number of periods necessary to repay the loan. You can see exactly what effect this will have on your payment schedule by using the NPER function, which returns the number of periods required to pay off a loan.

| D3 | ▾ | : | ✕ | ✓ | fx | =NPER(Monthly_Interest,Adjusted_Payment,Amount) | | | |

▲	A	B	C	D	E	F	G	H	I
1	Monthly Interest	0.4167%		($1,073.64)	Calculated Payment				
2	Months	360		($1,500.00)	Adjusted Payment				
3	Amount	$200,000		195	Adjusted Loan Term				
4	Payment Number	180							
5									
6									

> **Tip** Payments are considered cash outflows, so the result of a payment function is always negative. If you don't need the negative number for other calculations, you can display a positive payment amount by entering a minus sign between the equal sign and the function name in the formula, as in =-PMT(.4167,360,200000).

Calculating depreciation

Depreciation is a crucial tax calculation that allows businesses to spread tax deductions for major asset purchases over time, rather than having to expense them all in a single year. The United States Internal Revenue Service provides guidelines for the depreciable life of different classes of assets, and these are subject to change (see *IRS.gov* for details.) For example, cars are considered 5-year assets for tax purposes, whereas fruit trees are considered 10-year assets.

The depreciation functions in Excel include the declining-balance depreciation functions DB, DDB (double-declining), and VDB (variable-declining); the straight-line depreciation function SLN; and the sum-of-the-year's-digits depreciation function SYD. The following shows the syntax of the depreciation functions; non-italic arguments are required.

=SLN(cost, salvage, life)

=SYD(cost, salvage, life, per)

=DB(cost, salvage, life, period, month)

=DDB(cost, salvage, life, period, factor)

=VDB(cost, salvage, life, start_period, end_period, factor, no_switch)

Arguments common to the depreciation functions include those in the following table.

Argument	Description
Cost	The initial cost of the asset.
Life	The depreciable life of the asset.
Period	The period to be computed.

Argument	Description
Salvage	The residual value of the asset after depreciation.
No_switch	Used in the VDB function only. If omitted, the calculation switches to straight-line depreciation if the amount is greater than the declining balance calculation. If TRUE, does not switch.

Straight-line depreciation is calculated by chopping the total cost into equal pieces after subtracting the salvage value (the estimated market value of the asset at the end of its depreciable life).

When you calculate straight-line depreciation, however, the function returns the depreciation you can take for each period, which is the same for each period. The three declining balance methods (DB, DDB, and VDB) and the Sum-of-the-year's-digits method (SYD) calculate depreciation at accelerated rates. These depreciation functions require you to specify a period number because the amount of depreciation differs in each period.

Analyzing securities

Securities analysis is complex, and understanding the theories behind it is equally complex. T-bills mature in one year or less, and do not pay periodic interest, only interest at maturity. T-notes mature in 2 to 10 years, pay a semiannual coupon amount, and come in denominations of $100. There are TIPS and STRIPS and zero-coupon bonds, US Savings bonds, corporate bonds, and other types of securities that use similar mechanisms. Excel provides functions to massage them all.

The securities-analysis functions in Excel are located on the Financial menu in the Function Library group on the Formulas tab, and perform the following types of calculations:

- **DOLLARDE and DOLLARFR** Convert the typical fractional pricing of securities between fractional and decimal values

- **ACCRINT and ACCRINTM** Calculate the accrued interest for securities that accrue on either a periodic basis or at maturity

- **INTRATE and RECEIVED** Calculate either the interest rate or the total value at maturity for fully invested securities

- **PRICE, PRICEMAT, and PRICEDISC** Calculate the price for securities per $100 of face value, for securities that pay periodic interest, interest at maturity, or are discounted instead of paying periodic interest

- **YIELD, YIELDDISC, and YIELDMAT** Calculate the annual yield for securities that pay periodic interest, interest at maturity, or are discounted instead of paying periodic interest

- **DISC** Calculates the discount rate for a security

- **TBILLEQ, TBILLPRICE, and TBILLYIELD** Calculate yield, price, and bond-equivalent yield for US Treasury bills

- **COUPDAYBS, COUPDAYS, COUPDAYSNC, COUPNCD, COUPNUM, and COUPPCD** Calculate the number of coupons payable, and various associated dates and durations

- **DURATION and MDURATION** Calculate how bond prices responds to changes in yield

Arguments common to the securities analysis functions include those listed in the following table.

Argument	Description
Basis	The number of days in a year, as calculated. Default is 0=US (NASD) 30/360; 1=actual/actual; 2=actual/360; 3=actual/365; 4=European 30/360.
Coupon	The annual coupon rate of the security.
Frequency	The number of coupon payments per year: 1=annual; 2=semiannual; 4=quarterly.
Investment	The amount invested in the security.
Issue	The security's issue date.
Maturity	The date that the security matures.
Par	The face value of the security.
Price	The price of the security.
Rate	The interest rate of the security; must be greater than or equal to zero.
Redemption	The value of the security at redemption.
Settlement	The settlement date (date of payment) for the security.
Yield	The annual yield of the security.

> **Tip** A coupon, in bond terms, is an interest payment. Historically, bonds were physical certificates with tear-off coupons that you presented in exchange for a scheduled payment. This is where the term "coupon-clipper" originated.

These are very specialized functions that both require and extract specific details about the security you're investigating. For example, you can use the ACCRINT function to learn the amount of interest that has accrued by a security such as a US Treasury bond as of a certain date.

D1	▼	:	×	✓	fx	=ACCRINT(B1,B2,B3,B4,B5,B6,B7)			

	A	B	C	D	E	F	G	H
1	Issue	3/1/2014		1.416667				
2	First Interest	9/1/2014						
3	Settlement	4/1/2014						
4	Rate	0.017						
5	Par	1000						
6	Frequency	2						
7	Basis	0						
8								

➤ **To insert a financial function**

1. On the **Formulas** tab, in the **Function Library** group, click **Financial**, and then select the function you need.

2. In the **Function Arguments** dialog box, enter the arguments for the function.

Practice tasks

The practice files for these tasks are located in the MOSExcel2013Expert\Objective3 practice file folder. Save the results of the tasks in the same folder.

- Open the *ExcelExpert_3-1a* workbook and try performing the following tasks:
  - On Sheet1, insert a new column between columns G and H, and create a column of IF formulas that specify a different team and division.
  - On Sheet2, copy the shaded area and paste a copy below it. Edit the six formulas (and the labels) to include only team numbers above 4.
- Open the *ExcelExpert_3-1b* workbook and try performing the following tasks:
  - On the Periods worksheet, create a new formula to calculate the interest portion of payment number 175.
  - On the Securities worksheet, create a new ACCRINTM formula by using a basis of 1.

3.2 Look up data by using functions

Lookup functions are data-mining minions. You use them to address tables of data, searching for a particular value to display or use in a formula. The Lookup and Reference menu on the Formulas tab includes 19 functions, but this section focuses on the top contenders: LOOKUP, VLOOKUP, and HLOOKUP. The section also examines the TRANSPOSE function, which you use to flip vertically oriented data horizontal, and vice-versa.

Using the VLOOKUP and HLOOKUP functions

How to choose between the VLOOKUP and HLOOKUP functions depends upon how your table is organized. If your data is arranged in columns (labels on the left), use VLOOKUP. If your data is arranged in rows (labels at the top), use HLOOKUP. The following shows the syntax of these functions; non-italic arguments are required.

=*VLOOKUP(*lookup_value, table_array, col_index_num, *range_lookup)*

=*HLOOKUP(*lookup_value, table_array, row_index_num, *range_lookup)*

The *table_array* argument can be a range address or a name that defines the entire lookup table. The *col_index_num* and *row_index_num* arguments literally specify the column or row number in the table, counted from the top or left (including labels), from which to select the result. The *lookup_value* is the value that you want to match (approximately) in your table's row or column of comparison values.

> **Important** LOOKUP, VLOOKUP, and HLOOKUP normally look for the *greatest value that is less than or equal to the lookup value*, not necessarily an exact match. For this reason, the table must be sorted in ascending order, on the row or column that contains your comparison values. For example, if your *lookup_value* is 1,000 and the largest comparison value is 500, then the function returns 500. If, instead, you need to find an exact match, set the optional *range_lookup* argument to FALSE (0).

For example, the formula =*VLOOKUP(410,B3:D7,3)* looks in the first column of a 3 × 5 table in the range B3:D7, finds the greatest value that is less than or equal to 410 (400), and returns Epsilon, the value found in the third column of the table.

D1	▾	⋮	×	✓	*fx*	=VLOOKUP(410,B3:D7,3)		

⊿	A	B	C	D	E	F	G
1				Epsilon			
2							
3		100	123.45	Alpha			
4		200	23.45	Beta			
5		300	67.89	Delta			
6		400	234.56	Epsilon			
7		500	78.90	Gamma			
8							

If you edit the formula to include a value of 0 (FALSE) as the optional *range_lookup* argument, as in =*VLOOKUP(410,B3:D7,3,0)*, the result of the formula would be #N/A because there is not an exact match for 410 in the first column.

Similarly, the formula =*HLOOKUP("Beta",A3:D8,3)* looks in the first row of a 4 × 6 table in the range A3:D8, finds the greatest value that is less than or equal to Beta, and then returns the value found in the third row of the table.

D1	▾	⋮	×	✓	*fx*	=HLOOKUP("Beta",A3:D8,3)		

⊿	A	B	C	D	E	F	G
1				101			
2							
3	Alpha	Beta	Delta	Epsilon			
4	5	100	99	1			
5	10	101	98	2			
6	25	105	95	3			
7	30	110	94	2			
8	35	125	90	1			
9							

The text *Beta* happens to be an exact match. But if a text lookup value is not an exact match, the same rules apply. For example, if you misspell *Beta* in the previous formula to read =*HLOOKUP("Bata",A3:D8,3)*, the result of the function is 10 instead of 101 because, alphabetically, Alpha is the greatest value that is less than or equal to the lookup value Bata.

> **Tip** Uppercase and lowercase text are equivalent in lookup functions.

Using the LOOKUP function

You use the LOOKUP function primarily for one-dimensional lookup tasks—single rows or columns of data. You can also use LOOKUP with two-dimensional tables, but it always looks at the first row or column for the comparison value and selects the result from the same position in the last row or column. (You can specify any row or column by using VLOOKUP and HLOOKUP.)

The LOOKUP function has two forms. Use the *vector* form to return a value from a single row or column of data, or use the *array* form with either horizontally or vertically oriented tables. The following shows the syntax of the two forms.

=LOOKUP(lookup_value, lookup_vector, result_vector)

=LOOKUP(lookup_value, array)

As with the other lookup functions, you must sort your table in ascending order on the row or column that contains the comparison value. For example, the formula =LOOKUP("Delta",B3:B7,E3:E7) specifies a *lookup_vector* and an optional *result_vector* (both must be the same size). If a *result_vector* is not specified, the result is pulled from the *lookup_vector*.

E1			X	✓	ƒx	=LOOKUP("Delta",B3:B7,E3:E7)

	A	B	C	D	E	F	G
1					300		
2							
3		Alpha			100		
4		Beta			200		
5		Delta			300		
6		Epsilon			400		
7		Gamma			500		
8							

A7			X	✓	ƒx	=LOOKUP("Delta",A1:A5,C6:G6)

	A	B	C	D	E	F	G	H
1	Alpha							
2	Beta							
3	Delta							
4	Epsilon							
5	Gamma							
6			100	200	300	400	500	
7	300							
8								

The array form of the LOOKUP function automatically determines the orientation of the two-dimensional table specified by the *array* argument. If the table is wider than it is tall, LOOKUP searches the first row for a comparison value; if the table is taller than it is wide, (or square) it searches the first column. For most uses, it is best to use VLOOKUP or HLOOKUP, which allow more control and are easier to audit because the table orientation is indicated by the function name. LOOKUP is provided primarily for compatibility with other spreadsheet programs.

Using the TRANSPOSE function

The TRANSPOSE function does a seemingly simple thing (until you try to do it yourself): it flips the horizontal/vertical orientation of a selected range.

The tricks with this function are as follows:

- The formula must be entered as an array.

- Prior to entering the function, you must select a range to accept the transposed data that is exactly the same size as the source range, transposed.

When you lock in an array formula, the formula is duplicated in all selected cells, and brackets appear around the formula in the formula bar. You cannot edit any individual cell in an array; you must edit all cells in an array together. If you try editing a cell, Excel displays an error message. To edit an array, double-click any formula, edit it, and then press Ctrl+Shift+Enter again. This changes all the formulas in the array at once.

> **Tip** You can also transpose by clicking the Transpose button on the Paste Special button of the Home tab. After you copy the range you want to transpose and select the cell where you want the transposed range to start, click the Transpose button. Excel determines the orientation of the selected cells, and pastes them in the opposite orientation.

➤ **To insert a TRANSPOSE function**

1. On the **Formulas** tab, in the **Function Library** group, click **Lookup & Reference** and then click **TRANSPOSE**.

2. In the **Function Arguments** dialog box, specify the cell range you want to transpose.

➤ **To transpose a selected cell range**

1. Copy the range you want to transpose, and then click the cell where you want the result to start.

2. On the **Home** tab, in the **Clipboard** group, click the **Paste Special** button, and then click the **Transpose** icon in the **Paste** category.

   Or

1. Select a destination range that has exactly the same dimensions as the source range (transposed).

2. Enter a formula by using the TRANSPOSE function, specifying the source range.

3. Lock in the formula as an array by pressing **Ctrl+Shift+Enter**.

➤ **To insert a LOOKUP function**

1. On the **Formulas** tab, in the **Function Library** group, click **Lookup & Reference**, and then click the function you want.

2. In the **Function Arguments** dialog box, enter the function's arguments.

➤ **To enter an array formula**

→ Enter the formula, and then press **Ctrl+Shift+Enter**.

➤ **To edit an array formula**

→ Edit any formula in the array, and then press **Ctrl+Shift+Enter**.

Practice tasks

The practice file for these tasks is located in the MOSExcel2013Expert\Objective3 practice file folder. Save the results of the tasks in the same folder.

Open the *ExcelExpert_3_2* workbook and try performing the following tasks:

- ⊠ Edit the formula on the Vlookup worksheet so that the result is Beta.
- ⊠ Edit the formula on the Hlookup worksheet so that the result is 98.
- ⊠ On the Transpose worksheet, transpose the values in B10:F10.

3.3 Apply advanced date and time functions

Date and time arithmetic has its own rules and syntax. In Excel (and in most modern computers), date and time counting begins at 12:00 AM on January 1, 1900, starting at 1. January 2, 1900 is 2, and January 1, 2014 is 41640. Time is expressed as a decimal value expressing how much of the day has passed by. For example, the serial date 41640.50 is another way of saying "noon on New Year's Day 2014."

> **Tip** You can change the date or time value displayed in a cell to a serial date value by applying the General format. Click General in the Number Format list in the Number group on the Home tab. Click Short Date or Long Date to change it back again.

Fortunately, you don't have to enter dates that way, nor do you generally need to apply date or time formats. If you enter dates and times by using standard formats, Excel recognizes them and formats them automatically. For example, if you enter 1/1/14 into a cell, Excel correctly assumes you have entered a date, and applies the equivalent of the Short Date format (on the Number Format list), displaying 1/1/2014; Excel just expands the year from 14 to 2014, so that there is no confusion about the century. But when you select the cell and look in the formula bar, Excel displays the full date and time, not a serial date value like 41640. In fact, regardless of any additional date or time formatting that you apply, the formula bar display stays the same.

A2	▼	:	✕	✓	ƒx	1/1/2014 12:00:00 PM		

◢	A	B	C	D	E
1	1/1/2014	Short Date format			
2	Wednesday, January 1, 2014	Long Date format			
3	41640.5	General format			
4					
5					

Using the NOW and TODAY functions

The NOW and TODAY functions are as easy as it gets. Neither function takes a single argument; enter them, add a set of parentheses, and you're done. When you enter *=TODAY()* into a cell, the current date is displayed; when you enter *=NOW()* into a cell, the current date and time are displayed. And yes, you must enter both parentheses, or Excel displays an error message.

Both of these functions are *volatile*. This means that each time you open the workbook or edit a worksheet, the functions recalculate, displaying the date and/or time at that moment. Normally, formulas only recalculate when necessary; volatile functions recalculate at every available opportunity.

You can use these functions to insert starting dates or times into formulas that perform time-based calculations such as amortization or securities analysis.

B1	▼	:	✕	✓	ƒx	=TODAY()	

◢	A	B	C	D	E	F	G
1	Issue	6/16/2013		1.463889	Accrued Interest		
2	First Interest	12/17/2013					
3	Settlement	7/17/2013					
4	Rate	0.017					
5	Par	1000					
6	Frequency	2					
7	Basis	0					
8							
9							

Using functions to serialize dates and times

When using date and time functions, Excel always calculates by using the precise under-lying serial values. But when constructing formulas, you might need only the month or a specific time of day. Or you might need to convert imported dates that have been stored as text into dates that Excel recognizes. Excel includes a suite of functions you can use to address these tasks, and more.

Using the YEAR, MONTH, DAY, HOUR, MINUTE, and SECOND functions

The YEAR, MONTH, DAY, HOUR, MINUTE, and SECOND functions each extract only the corresponding component of a date or time. They all accept just a single argument, which can be a reference to a cell that contains a date or time value, another date or time function, or a text date enclosed in quotation marks, as in =YEAR("1/1/2014").

Using the DATEVALUE and TIMEVALUE functions

The DATEVALUE and TIMEVALUE functions convert text dates and times into serial values, which is generally not necessary because Excel recognizes dates in most configurations. But sometimes they can come in handy when building formulas that use other formu-las, or if you need to work with imported, unformatted text. Again, these functions take but a single argument, a reference to a cell that contains a date value, a date in text surrounded by quotes, or another date or time function. For example, the formula =DATEVALUE("December 13, 2014") returns the serial date value 41986. You can also use these functions to construct dates. For example, the formula =DATEVALUE(C2&"-"&C3&"-"&C1) returns a serial date value based on the values contained in the referenced cells (assuming they contain valid date values). A text-style date is constructed within the function by using cell references separated by dashes. In effect, the function first interprets the text, and then converts the date.

| E2 | ▾ | : | ✕ | ✓ | fx | =DATEVALUE(C2&"-"&C3&"-"&C1) |

⊿	A	B	C	D	E	F
1	Sunday, June 16, 2013 12:57 PM	Year	2013		41986	
2		Month	6		41441	
3		Day	16			
4		Hour	12			
5		Minute	57			
6		Second	55			
7						
8						

Concatenating text in formulas

Concatenation is the linking of characters or strings in a specific order to form a single string. The concatenation operator is the ampersand (&). You can use concatenation to construct arguments within a function, or to merge the contents of cells. The process is simple: when you want to add a string of text, enclose it in ampersands. For example, the formula *=(DATEVALUE(11&"/"&12&"/"&13)* uses ampersands to construct the text string 11/12/13. Each number is connected by a *&"/"&* statement. The ampersand instructs Excel that what follows is to be inserted as text: if a cell reference, the cell value is inserted; if text, it must be enclosed in quotation marks. The concatenation operator can be used in formulas without functions as well. For example, if cell A1 contains the text *Jelly* and cell A2 contains the text *Donut*, the formula *=A1&A2* returns the text string *JellyDonut*. To add a space, the formula *=A1&" "&A2* does the trick. The space character must be enclosed in quotation marks, which is in turn enclosed in ampersands. You can also use the CONCATENATE function, which takes the form *=CONCATENATE (Text1, Text2, ...).*

Using the WEEKDAY, WORKDAY, and NETWORKDAYS functions

The WEEKDAY, WORKDAY, and NETWORKDAYS functions are helpful when calculating work or payroll schedules, planning projects, or even planning a vacation. The WEEKDAY function can be used to determine the day of the week for a specific date, and returns a value from 1 through 7. The function takes the form *=WEEKDAY(serial_number, return_type)*, where *serial_number* is a date value or reference to a cell containing a date. *Return_type* is an optional argument indicating the way the days are counted. The default *return_type* is 1, indicating that 1=Sunday and 7=Saturday; a value of 1 indicates that 1=Monday and 7=Sunday; and a value of 3 specifies a number from 0 through 6, where 0=Monday and 6=Sunday.

> **Tip** You can add or subtract days from a date by using + and – signs. For example, if cell B1 contains 1/1/2013, the formula =*B1+1* returns 1/2/2013.

The WORKDAY function takes the form =*WORKDAY(start_date, days, holidays)* and returns a date that is a specified number of *days* before or after a given *start_date,* excluding weekends and (optionally) holidays. The NETWORKDAYS function counts the number of workdays between two dates, and takes them from =*NETWORKDAYS(start_date, end_date, holidays)*. For both functions, *holidays* is an optional argument specifying a list of dates that you want to exclude.

The WORKDAY.INTL and NETWORKDAYS.INTL functions each take an additional argument—*weekend*—that specifies alternate days of the week to use as nonwork days. A list of options appears when you select the *weekend* argument while editing the NETWORKDAYS.INTL function. Just click one of the 17 different combinations of weekend days (days off) to insert the corresponding number (for example, if you click the 7 - Friday, Saturday option, the number 7 is inserted into the function).

	A	B	C			J	K	L
CONCATE... ▼ : × ✓ *fx*			=NETWORKDAYS.INTL(B1,B3,)					
				NETWORKDAYS.INTL(start_date, end_date, [weekend], [holidays])		Saturday and Sunday are weekend days		
1	Start date	1/1/2013	10/23/2017 Workday	1 - Saturday, Sunday				
2	Number of Days	1,234	863 Networkdays	2 - Sunday, Monday				
3	End Date	5/19/2016	9/25/2017 Workday.intl	3 - Monday, Tuesday				
4			ITL(B1,B3,) Networkdays.in	4 - Tuesday, Wednesday				
5	Holidays			5 - Wednesday, Thursday				
6	1/1/2014			6 - Thursday, Friday				
7	1/20/2014			7 - Friday, Saturday				
8	2/17/2014			11 - Sunday only				
9	5/26/2014			12 - Monday only				
10	7/4/2014			13 - Tuesday only				
11	9/1/2014			14 - Wednesday only				
12	10/13/2014			15 - Thursday only				
13	11/11/2014							
14	11/27/2014							
15	12/25/2014							
16	1/1/2015							
17	1/19/2015							

> **Tip** Your list of holidays would be best located on its own worksheet in the workbook.

> **To insert a NOW or TODAY function**

→ On the **Formulas** tab, in the **Function Library** group, click the **Date & Time** button, click **NOW** or **TIME**, and then click **OK**.

➤ **To insert a DATEVALUE or TIMEVALUE function**

1. On the **Formulas** tab, in the **Function Library** group, click the **Date & Time** button, and then click **DATEVALUE** or **TIMEVALUE**.

2. In the **Function Arguments** dialog box, enter the text or reference you want to convert.

Practice tasks

The practice file for these tasks is located in the MOSExcel2013Expert\Objective3 practice file folder. Save the results of the tasks in the same folder.

Open the *ExcelExpert_3_3* workbook and try performing the following tasks:

- ☒ On the Work worksheet, create a new NETWORKDAYS.INTL formula where Sunday and Monday are considered weekends.

- ☒ On the Concat worksheet, create a new CONCATENATE formula that assembles the words in column B into a sentence.

3.4 Create scenarios

In Excel, a *scenario* is a selection of cells that contain specific values you can save and reapply at any time. To create one, use the Scenario Manager, which is described later in this section. In a broader context, a scenario is a possible world; a collection of assumptions about the future; a guideline you can use to prepare for the worst case, the best case, or anything in between. Each line item in an annual budget could have multiple scenarios, for example, depending on the planners' perception of what the future holds.

This section first provides values with which to populate scenarios by using what-if analysis tools. Then it describes how to consolidate data from multiple worksheets into one.

Strategy The objective domain for Microsoft Office Specialist Expert Exam 77-428, "MOS Excel 2013 Expert, Part 2" includes "Using financial functions" as a topic under Objective 3.4. This topic appears in section 3.1, "Apply functions in formulas."

Using what-if analysis tools

By using built-in tools that appear on the What-If Analysis menu in the Data Tools group on the Data tab, you can calculate a value for a variable that helps you meet a goal, define and run scenarios, and test a range of values for one or two variables by using a data table. Also on the Data tab, the Solver add-in can be used to tackle larger models with multiple variables.

Simply stated, what-if analysis is changing one or more variables in a data model to test a range of possible results. Suppose you want to predict an inevitable rise in the cost of materials by using a range of percentages, such as -2%, +5% or +15%, which can represent "best case, likely case, worst case." Use what-if analysis to try different options, and use the Scenario Manager to keep track of the results.

Using Goal Seek

The Goal Seek feature, which you access from the What-If Analysis menu in the Data Tools group on the Data tab, helps you obtain a specific result, using a single variable. In the Goal Seek dialog box, you point to a cell that contains a formula (called the *set cell*), enter the value you are seeking, and then specify the changing cell—the cell whose value Excel changes to meet the goal you define.

> **Tip** If you work with what-if analysis tools, you'll find it helpful to name cells and cell ranges rather than use cell references (for example, Revenue instead of $D$12). To name a cell or cell range, select it and then enter a name in the name box to the left of the formula bar. Names cannot include spaces and must be unique within a workbook.

The Step and Pause buttons in the Goal Seek Status dialog box are enabled when Excel needs many calculation iterations to find the goal. Use the Pause button to pause the calculation, and click Step to proceed through each iteration one at a time.

Enabling iterative calculations

If you pose a particularly challenging goal-seeking problem, Excel might be unable to arrive at a precise solution, particularly if there are any circular references involved. Circular references are formulas that loop back on themselves through other formulas, which is usually not desirable, but is not uncommon in complex what-if models. Enabling iterative calculation can help. To do so, click Options in the Backstage view, and click Formulas. In the Calculation Options section of the Excel Options dialog box, select the Enable Iterative Calculation check box. The default but adjustable settings are 100 iterations with a maximum change value of .001. If, within the given number of iterations, Excel comes within the maximum change value of your goal, calculation stops and the result is displayed.

➤ **To identify a goal by using Goal Seek**

1. Select the cell that contains the formula you want to solve for.

2. On the **Data** tab, in the **Data Tools** group, click **What-If Analysis**, and then click **Goal Seek**.

3. Enter your goal in the **To value** box.

4. In the **By changing cell** box, specify the cell where you want the result to appear.

Using Solver

Solver is designed to find an optimal value by manipulating multiple variables and combinations of variables. You can additionally specify multiple conditions that must be met in order to achieve a solution.

In a Solver model, you need to define three basic elements:

- An objective or target, which is the value you want to optimize

- Changing cells, which are the values you can adjust to reach the objective

- Constraints, which are conditions that must be met in evaluating the model

For example, in a model projecting sales and cost of goods sold for a group of products who share a common production budget, one goal could be to find a balance between cost and sales volume that optimizes the production budget costs. If it were that simple, however, you could just sell a zillion units of your most profitable product; an unrealistic solution that an unconstrained optimization would likely produce.

So, you can use the Solver to keep everything within parameters, such as the following:

- The grand total of the product group's cost of goods cannot exceed $150,000.
- The minimum projected sales per product is 50 units.
- No single product can consume more than 20 percent of the grand total.
- The cost of products 4 and 5 together cannot exceed $35,000.
- Projected sales must be expressed in integers.

> **Tip** Before using the Solver, name the cells and cell ranges you'll be working with, to make them easier to read and to work with.

	A	B	C	D	E	F	G	H
1	Constraints				*Total supply budget - Alpha*		$150,000	
2					*Total budget for Product 4 + 5*		$35,000	
3					*Maximum % of budget spent on any product*		20.00%	
4					*Minimum sales per product*		50	
5	**Product Group** **Alpha**	**Cost of** **Goods**	**Profit** **margin**	**Projected** **Sales**	**Total** **Profit**	**Total Cost**	**Percent** **of total**	
6	Product 1	$55.87	11.50%	250	$1,606	$13,968	9%	
7	Product 2	$103.00	8.40%	250	$2,163	$25,750	16%	
8	Product 3	$8.45	8.20%	250	$173	$2,113	1%	
9	Product 4	$183.66	11.20%	250	$5,142	$45,915	28%	
10	Product 5	$288.00	13.90%	250	$10,008	$72,000	44%	
11	Product 6	$16.99	16.30%	250	$692	$4,248	3%	
12	Total Cost of Goods						$163,993	
13	Product 4 + 5 only						$117,915	
14								

Solver Parameters

Se_t Objective: GrandTotal

To: ○ Ma_x   ● Mi_n   ○ _Value Of: 0

_By Changing Variable Cells:
Projected_Sales

Su_bject to the Constraints:
GrandTotal <= $G$1
Projected_Sales >= $G$4
Products4and5only <= $G$2
Percent_of_total <= $G$3
Projected_Sales = integer

A_dd
_Change
_Delete
_Reset All
_Load/Save

☐ Ma_ke Unconstrained Variables Non-Negative

S_elect a Solving Method: GRG Nonlinear

O_ptions

Solving Method
Select the GRG Nonlinear engine for Solver Problems that are smooth nonlinear. Select the LP Simplex engine for linear Solver Problems, and select the Evolutionary engine for Solver problems that are non-smooth.

_Help   _Solve   Cl_ose

Add Constraint

C_ell Reference: Co_nstraint:
Percent_of_total   <=   =$G$3

_OK   A_dd   _Cancel

When you set up constraints, you can specify that a cell or cell range must be a whole number by choosing *Int* (integer) from the list of operators. You can specify *Bin* (binary) as the constraint type to set up yes/no decisions, or *Dif* to specify a constraint to indicate that all the values in the constrained cell or cells are different. In the Add Constraint dialog box, you can also enter values directly into the Constraint box.

Solver provides three options in the Select A Solving Method list in the Solver Parameters dialog box:

- **GRG Nonlinear** This is the default method, which applies to nonlinear problems whose points sit on a line that is curved.

- **Simplex LP** Use this method for straight-line problems.

- **Evolutionary** This method applies to problems whose elements do not fit on either a straight or curved line (that is, the elements are more random or discontinuous).

In the Solver Options dialog box, you can set options for solving limits (maximum time and number of iterations), that let you step through each iteration of Solver's calculations (Show Iteration Results), and provides an option that controls the precision of values that are under constraints. The default value for precision is 0.000001. Changing the precision to a lower amount (closer to 1) might result in additional time needed to solve a problem.

> **Important** When the Solver Results dialog box appears on the screen, it might be in front of your data. The results are on the worksheet already, so take a look before you commit to keeping the results. You can drag the dialog box out of the way. If you click OK to keep the solution Solver arrived at, the results remain on the worksheet, and cannot be undone.

When you save a workbook in which you have defined a problem for Solver, Excel saves the Solver information with the workbook. You can store one set of Solver parameters with each worksheet in a workbook; however, you can store and retrieve additional sets by clicking the Load/Save button in the Solver Parameters dialog box.

> **Tip** This section is a brief introduction to Solver. To learn more about the details of how to work with Solver and the type of problems it can analyze, see the chapters about Solver in *Microsoft Excel 2010 Data Analysis and Business Modeling* by Wayne Winston (Microsoft Press, 2010). You can also find information at *www.solver.com*.

Using the watch window

In the watch window, you can keep an eye on critical formulas as you edit the worksheet. Rather than having to jump back and forth between locations on a worksheet or between workbooks, you can keep the formulas you need to see in view.

Click the Watch Window command in the Formula Auditing group on the Formulas tab. Then select the cell or cells you want to keep an eye on. When you click Add Watch, Excel adds an entry to the watch window that lists the workbook, worksheet, cell reference, value, and any formula that's defined in that cell. As you edit, the effects of your edits are reflected in real time in the watch window. You can also dock the watch window by dragging it to the top, bottom, or sides of the worksheet window.

Watch Window   ▾ ✕
🔲 Add Watch...   🔲 Delete Watch

Book	Sheet	Name	Cell	Value	Formula
CostAnalysis.xlsx	Sheet1	Products4and5only	F13	$117,915	=F9+F10
CostAnalysis.xlsx	Sheet1	TotalCost	F12	$163,993	=SUM(F6:F11)

Formulas that you add to the watch window are saved with the workbook, and continue to be available until you select them and click **Delete Watch**.

➤ **To load the Solver add-in**

1. In the **Backstage** view, click **Options**.

2. In the **Excel Options** dialog box, click **Add-Ins**.

3. In the **Manage** list, click **Excel Add-ins**, and then click **Go**.

4. In the **Add-Ins** dialog box, select the **Solver Add-in** check box, and then click **OK**.

➤ **To set up Solver parameters**

1. On the **Data** tab, in the **Analysis** group, click **Solver**.

2. In the **Solver Parameters** dialog box, specify the **Set Objective** cell.

3. In the **To** area, select **Max**, **Min**, or **Value Of**. If you choose **Value Of**, enter a value.

4. In the **By Changing Variable Cells** box, specify the cells whose values Solver can change when analyzing the data.

5. In the **Subject to the Constraints** area, click **Add**, and then define the constraint in the **Add Constraint** dialog box. Click **Add** in the **Add Constraint** dialog box to define another constraint. Click **OK** when you finish defining constraints.

6. Click **Solve**.

Using the Scenario Manager

To manage your what-if models so that you recall them instantly, use the Scenario Manager. You can create multiple scenarios by using the same model, for example, Best, Most Likely, or Worst Case. Each scenario can store values for up to 32 changing cells. For example, after making changes to a Solver model, you could save the result as a scenario named *Solved*.

	A	B	C	D	E	F	G	H	I	J	K	L	M
1	Constraints					Total supply budget - Alpha	$150,000						
2						Total budget for Product 4 + 5	$35,000			Add Scenario		?	x
3					Maximum % of budget spent on any product		20.00%						
4						Minimum sales per product	50	Scenario name:					
5	Product Group Alpha	Cost of Goods	Profit margin	Projected Sales	Total Profit	Total Cost	Percent of total	Solved					
6	Product 1	$55.87	11.50%	250	$1,604	$13,948	19%	Changing cells: D6:D11					
7	Product 2	$103.00	8.40%	124	$1,072	$12,758	18%	Ctrl+click cells to select non-adjacent changing cells.					
8	Product 3	$8.45	8.20%	490	$339	$4,136	6%	Comment:					
9	Product 4	$183.66	11.20%	78	$1,613	$14,400	20%	Created by Mark on 6/18/2013					
10	Product 5	$288.00	13.90%	50	$2,002	$14,400	20%						
11	Product 6	$16.99	16.30%	727	$2,014	$12,358	17%						
12	Total Cost of Goods					$72,000		Protection					
13	Product 4 + 5 only					$28,800		✔ Prevent changes					
14								☐ Hide					
15													
16										OK		Cancel	

You define a scenario by specifying changing cells, whose value you want to record when you're done. Excel displays the Scenario Values dialog box, in which the current value is displayed for each of the changing cells you selected.

> **Tip** Consider selecting your changing cells before performing any analysis, and save them as a scenario named something like *Beginning* or *Original*. This makes it easy to start over if you don't like the results.

To edit a scenario, select it in the Scenario Manager and click Edit. Make any changes in the Edit Scenario dialog box and the Scenario Values dialog box, where you can modify the values for each changing cell directly.

Click the Show button in Scenario Manager to insert the values for the selected scenario in the worksheet.

Merging scenarios

You can distribute a workbook, have other people define scenarios in their copies of the workbook, and then merge them all into a single workbook. With the workbooks that contain scenarios open, click the Merge button in the Scenario Manager dialog box. In the Merge Scenario dialog box, select the workbook that contains the scenarios you want to merge.

➤ **To define a scenario and then view the results**

1. On the Data tab, in the **Data Tools** group, click **What-If Analysis**, and then click **Scenario Manager**.

2. In Scenario Manager, click **Add**.

3. In the **Add Scenario** dialog box, enter a name for the scenario.

4. In the **Changing cells** box, specify each cell you want to alter, and click **OK**.

5. In the **Scenario Values** dialog box, enter the values for each changing cell.

6. Click **Add** to define another scenario, or click **OK** to return to the **Scenario Manager** dialog box.

➤ **To see the results of a scenario**

→ In the **Scenario Manager** dialog box, select a scenario and click **Show**.

➤ **To edit a scenario**

1. In the **Scenario Manager** dialog box, select a scenario, and then click **Edit**.

2. In the **Edit Scenario** dialog box, change the scenario name or alter the list of changing cells. Then click **OK**.

3. In the **Scenario Values** dialog box, modify the values of changing cells.

➤ **To delete a scenario**

→ In Scenario Manager, select a scenario, and then click **Delete**.

Consolidating data

You can use the Consolidate command in the Data Tools group on the Data tab to combine values from up to 255 worksheets into one master worksheet. The source worksheets can be from the same workbook or from other workbooks, and the consolidation settings are saved so that you can rerun it at any time. You can consolidate data in two ways:

- **Consolidation by position** Using this command is the easiest way to consolidate, but the cell ranges in all supporting worksheets must be the same size with identical row and column labels in identical locations.

- **Consolidation by category** By using this command, you can collect data from supporting worksheets whose cell ranges are different sizes, but use the identical row and column labels in different locations.

Consolidating by position

Suppose you have three worksheets containing sales data—Jan, Feb, and Mar—and you want to create a quarterly summary. The layout and labels are identical in all three worksheets. With all the supporting worksheets open, the first step is to select cells on the empty summary sheet where you want the consolidated data to go, without selecting the row or column labels.

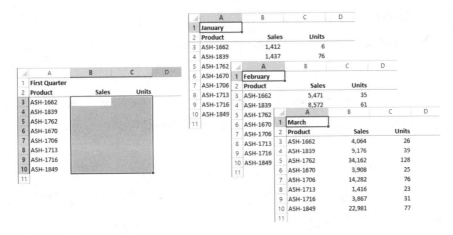

In the Consolidate dialog box, you specify a cell range to consolidate by clicking a worksheet tab (or a tab in another workbook) to activate it, and then dragging to select cells. References are inserted in the dialog box. In a consolidation by position, you shouldn't need to select cells again, just the worksheet tab, because Excel selects the same range of cells specified in the first consolidation reference.

Tip If you select row or column labels, click Use Labels In in the Consolidate dialog box so that the consolidated result includes them.

Repeat this process for each worksheet until all the cell ranges you want to consolidate are represented in the All References box. Consolidation data is saved with the workbook, so that the next time you use the Consolidate command, you can rerun the same consolidation immediately.

> **Tip** You can add sheets to a consolidation from other workbooks, but if they are not open you'll have to type external cell references from memory, including the full path to the folder. If you aren't working with too many sheets, hold down the Ctrl key while dragging a copy of each sheet into one workbook, and then run the consolidation there.

Consolidating by category

Suppose you have three similar worksheets you want to consolidate, but each contains different data in the rows and columns. This time when you consolidate, you'll include the labels from your source worksheets. The first step in this case is to select a single cell on the summary worksheet where you want the consolidated data to start. Make sure there is room; give the summary its own worksheet and you won't have to worry.

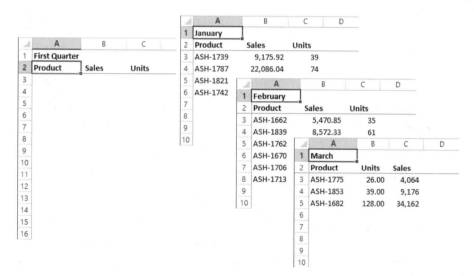

This time on the summary worksheet, just select a single cell specifying the upper-left corner of the result range. The consolidation will pull in values and the labels from the source worksheets. The Consolidate command uses the labels from each source sheet to put the results in the right places. If the row or column labels match, Excel adds the values together; if they are different, Excel adds another row or column.

In the Consolidate dialog box, you'll need to select each range manually to ensure that all the data you need makes it into the summary, because all the cell ranges are different sizes. Make sure to include both the row and column labels in all the selections.

	A	B	C
1	First Quarter		
2	Product	Sales	Units
3	ASH-1662	5,470.85	35
4	ASH-1839	8,572.33	61
5	ASH-1762	15,888.60	78
6	ASH-1670	19,786.20	70
7	ASH-1706	5,470.85	35
8	ASH-1713	3,867.50	50
9	ASH-1739	9,175.92	39
10	ASH-1787	22,086.04	74
11	ASH-1821	1,948.70	65
12	ASH-1742	7,358.06	79
13	ASH-1775	4,064	26.00
14	ASH-1853	9,176	39.00
15	ASH-1682	34,162	128.00

Consolidate dialog box:
Function: Sum
Reference: Browse...
All references:
Feb!$A$2:$C$8
Jan!$A$2:$C$6
Mar!$A$2:$C$5
Add / Delete
Use labels in: ☑ Top row ☑ Left column ☐ Create links to source data
OK   Close

Sheet tabs: Summary | Jan | Feb | Mar

Tip The consolidations discussed in this section are static; if the source data changes, you'll need to rerun the consolidation. But you can create a dynamic consolidation that updates automatically by clicking Create Links To Source Data in the Consolidate dialog box, which inserts reference formulas in your summary worksheet.

➤ **To consolidate data by position**

1. Open the workbook or workbooks to consolidate.
2. On the summary worksheet, select the range that will contain the consolidated data. This range and all the source ranges must be the same size, and all must have identical row and/or column labels.
3. On the **Data** tab, in the **Data Tools** group, click the **Consolidate** button.
4. Select the function that you want to apply, and then click in the **Reference** box.
5. Click the first worksheet tab you want to add, select the data you want to consolidate, and then click the **Add** button. Repeat for each worksheet you want to consolidate.
6. Select options for labels and links, if necessary.
7. Click **OK**.

➤ **To consolidate data by category**

1. Open the workbook or workbooks to consolidate.

2. On the summary worksheet, select the cell in the upper-left corner of the range that will contain the consolidated data.

3. On the **Data** tab, in the **Data Tools** group, click **Consolidate**.

4. Select the function that you want to apply, and then click in the **Reference** box.

5. Click the first worksheet tab you want to add, select the data you want to consolidate, and then click the **Add** button. Repeat for each worksheet you want to consolidate.

6. Select options for labels and links, if necessary.

7. Click **OK**.

Practice tasks

The practice files for these tasks are located in the MOSExcel2013Expert\Objective3 practice file folder. Save the results of the tasks in the same folder.

- Open the *ExcelExpert_3-4a* workbook and on the Goal Seek worksheet, find a price that would yield revenue of $125,000.

- Open the *ExcelExpert_3-4b* workbook and run the Solver; increase the cost of goods for products 4 and 5 by 10 percent and save the result as a new scenario.

- Open the *ExcelExpert_3-4c* workbook and consolidate values by position from the Jan, Feb, and Mar worksheets on the Summary sheet.

- Open the *ExcelExpert_3-4d* workbook and consolidate values by category from the Jan, Feb, and Mar worksheets on the Summary sheet. Add fake data to any or all of the month worksheets and rerun the consolidation.

Objective review

Before finishing this chapter, ensure that you have mastered the following skills:

3.1 Apply functions in formulas
3.2 Look up data by using functions
3.3 Apply advanced date and time functions
3.4 Create scenarios

4 Create advanced charts and tables

The skills tested in this section of the Microsoft Office Specialist Expert exams for Microsoft Excel 2013 relate to creating sophisticated charts and tables. Specifically, the following objectives are associated with this set of skills:

4.1 Create advanced chart elements

4.2 Create and manage PivotTables

4.3 Create and manage PivotCharts

The data contained in an Excel worksheet can often be presented as a chart for the purposes of analysis, reporting, and sharing. You can use charts to add emphasis in verbal presentations and printed reports, or to present data that is inherently visual or difficult to describe, such as a trend or a growth curve. Excel 2013 provides a variety of tools that you can use to create charts and tables to display your data.

This chapter guides in you studying methods for creating advanced chart elements, and creating and managing PivotTables and PivotCharts.

> **Practice Files** To complete the practice tasks in this chapter, you need the practice files contained in the MOSExcel2013Expert\Objective4 practice file folder. For more information, see "Download the practice files" in this book's Introduction.

4.1 Create advanced chart elements

This section describes specific features you can apply to charts to highlight trends in data, how to use chart templates. This section also explains how to plot chart data on more than one axis.

> **Tip** This section assumes you are familiar with techniques to create and format basic charts in Excel. If you need more information about creating charts, see the Excel Help topics listed under "Creating Charts" and "Formatting Charts."

Adding trendlines to charts

By using a trendline, you can examine the general movement of data over time. Trendlines are used in regression analysis, a type of statistical analysis in which a forecast is made by building a historical trendline and projecting it into the future. They rely on the *R-squared value*, a decimal value from 0 through 1 that indicates how closely the trendline corresponds to the actual data (the closer to 1 the better).

> **Tip** You can only add trendlines to certain chart types, including area, bar, column, and line charts. If you change a chart to a type that does not support them, Excel removes the trendlines.

The type and pattern of the data determines the type of trendline you should use. The following list summarizes the types of trendlines available in Excel:

- **Linear** A straight line, appropriate when data does not fluctuate much over time.

- **Logarithmic** A curved line, appropriate for data whose fluctuations tend to decrease over time; can use negative and positive values.

- **Polynomial** A line that can have multiple peaks and valleys; appropriate when data tends to fluctuate.

- **Power** A curved line, appropriate for data that tends to increase at a specific rate; must be positive values.

- **Exponential** A curved line, appropriate for values that rise or fall at constantly increasing rates; must be positive and nonzero.

- **Moving average** A line that can fluctuate and apply a variable amount of smoothing to a pattern or trend.

To apply a trendline to a chart, click the Trendline button on the Add Chart Element menu in the Chart Layouts group on the Design tool tab. You can point to an option on the Trendline menu to see the option previewed on the chart, and then click the one you like. Or, click More Trendline Options at the bottom of the menu to display the Format Trendline pane, which offers the same trendline types, but affords more control, including additional subpanes for Fill & Line and Effects.

For example, if you select the Polynomial trendline type, you can change the sensitivity of the trendline by adjusting the Order number. Polynomial and moving average trendlines calculate trends based on a given number of successive data points. You can adjust the amount of smoothing applied by using the Order control (Period control for moving average), starting at 2 points. Lower numbers make for smoother trendlines.

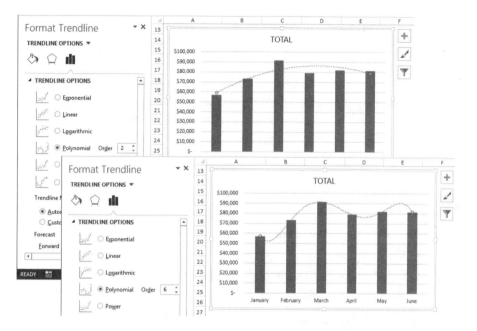

The Format Trendline pane has three subpanes, represented by the three icons near the top of the pane.

- **Trendline Options** Displayed when you first add a trendline or double-click an existing trendline

- **Fill & Line** Controls colors and the appearance of lines and arrows

- **Effects** Used for applying special Shadow, Glow, and Soft Edges object-formatting effects

In the Trendline Options pane, you can assign a different name, forecast into the past or the future, set the intercept (the point at which the trendline crosses the vertical axis, if applicable), and display the underlying equation and/or R-squared value on the chart, depending on the chart type.

> **See Also** For information about adding a slicer to a chart, see the "Creating slicers" topic in section 4.2, "Create and manage PivotTables."

Working with other elements

The Add Chart Element menu in the Chart Layouts group on the Design tool tab offers submenus full of other elements besides trendlines. Each submenu offers similar options that you access via the pane. The menus include Axes, Axis Titles, Chart Title, Data Labels, Data Table, Error Bars, Gridlines, Legend, Lines, Trendline, and Up/Down bars. For example, the Lines command draws "drop lines" that connect data points to the horizontal (category) axis. Applying drop lines can help clarify the location of data points. High-low lines extend from the highest value to the lowest value in each category. High-low lines appear by default in stock charts. Up-down bars show the difference between data points in a chart with more than one data series. After you insert any of these elements, you can double-click the element to edit it, which displays the associated pane.

➤ **To add a trendline**

1. Click the chart to select it, or select the individual data series to which you want to add a trendline.

2. On the **Design** tool tab, in the **Chart Layouts** group, click the **Add Chart Element** button, and then click **Trendline**.

3. Select the type of trendline, or click **More Trendline Options**, and then select the type of trendline you want to use in the **Format Trendlines** pane.

➤ **To change the format of a trendline**

1. On the chart, double-click the trendline you want to change.

2. Change options on the **Fill & Line**, **Effects**, and **Trendline Options** panes of the **Format Trendline** pane.

➤ **To specify the number of periods to include in a forecast**

1. On the chart, click the trendline you want to work with.

2. Click the **Add Chart Element** button, click **Trendline**, and then click **More Trendline Options**.

3. In the **Forecast** area of the **Format Trendline** pane, specify the number of periods in the **Forward** and **Backward** boxes.

➤ **To remove a trendline**

1. On the chart, select the trendline you want to remove.

2. Click the **Add Chart Element** button, click **Trendline**, and then click **None**, or simply press **Delete**.

Creating dual-axis charts

In some charts, the data you want to visualize is incongruous, such as stock prices and sales volume, which are often shown together on the same chart. Or you include data sets that are scaled orders of magnitude apart, such as comparing total sales next to sales of an individual salesperson. To handle examples such as these in a chart, you can add a second value axis for one of the sets of data. With a secondary value axis in place, you can add a second category (horizontal) axis. You can also change the chart type for the data series plotted on the secondary axis—for example, you can plot one set of data in a column chart and then change the data series on the secondary axis to a line chart.

In a chart with multiple data series, double-click the data series you want to plot on a secondary axis, which displays the Format Data Series pane.

> **Tip** You can apply a secondary axis only to a two-dimensional chart. You cannot apply secondary axes to three-dimensional charts.

The Secondary Axis option adds new data directly on top of the primary data, so you need to change the chart type in order to see it. Right-click the data series plotted on the secondary axis and choose Change Series Chart Type from the shortcut menu. At the bottom of the Change Chart Type dialog box, you can select a different chart type for each data series using the drop-down menus adjacent to each series name.

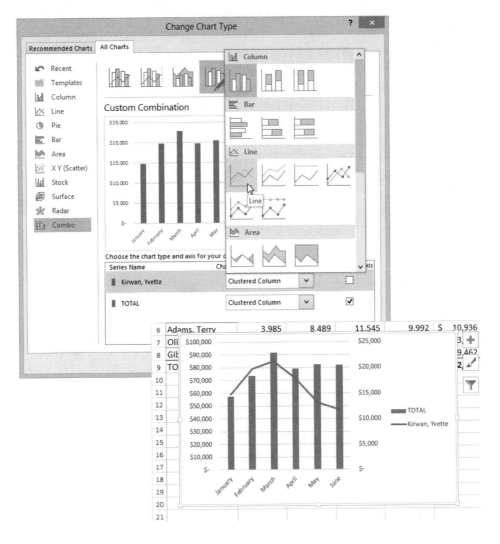

> **Tip** Be careful not to select a new chart type for an axis by using the chart types listed down the left side of the Change Chart Type dialog box. Changing one of these will change the entire chart, not just the selected data series.

You can add more data series to a two-axis chart, but you can't add more axes. On the Design tool tab, the Select Data button in the Data group opens a dialog box that has options you can use to select additional data sets to apply to the same chart. Then, you use the options in the Change Chart Type dialog box to assign the new data series to an axis. You can reverse the row/column order of your chart by using the Switch Row/ Column button in the dialog box, and add or edit legend entries and axis labels.

	A	B	C	D	E	F	G	H
1	Salesperson	January	February	March	April	May	June	TOTAL
2	Kirwan, Yvette	$ 14,753	$ 19,800	$ 21,294	$ 17,928	$ 13,109	$ 11,705	$ 98,589
3	Moore, Bobby	5,745	7,813	5,409	4,875	$ 1,773	$ 3,102	$ 28,717
4	Madigan, Tony	12,732	10,574	20,631	18,025	$ 23,736	$ 26,265	$ 111,963
5	Hedlund, Magnus	17,724	18,077	21,049	18,724	$ 19,686	$ 18,672	$ 113,932
6	Adams, Terry	3,985	8,489	11,545	9,992	$ 10,936	$ 11,245	$ 56,192
7	Oliviera, Manuel	2,334	8,761	4,125	3,548	$ 3,548	$ 4,879	$ 27,195
8	Gibbins, Phil	-	-	7,526	5,961	$ 9,462	$ 5,961	$ 28,910
9	TOTAL	$ 57,273	$ 73,514	$ 91,579	$ 79,053	$ 82,249	$ 81,829	$ 465,497

Select Data Source dialog box:

Chart data range: =Summary!$A$1:$G$2,Summary!$A$4:$G$4,Summary!$A$9:$G$9

Switch Row/Column

Legend Entries (Series)
- Add
- Edit
- Remove
  - ☑ Kirwan, Yvette
  - ☑ Madigan, Tony
  - ☑ TOTAL

Horizontal (Category) Axis Labels
- Edit
  - ☑ January
  - ☑ February
  - ☑ March
  - ☑ April
  - ☑ May

Hidden and Empty Cells   OK   Cancel

When you're done, the new series might be added to the wrong axis. To switch the data to the secondary axis, right-click the new series, click Change Series Chart Type, and then select a chart type to match the existing data series.

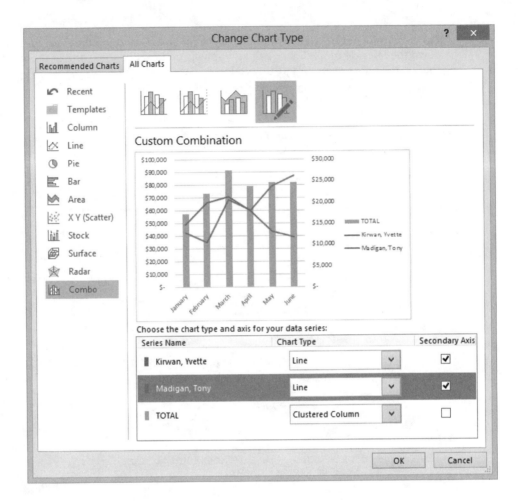

> ➤ **To add a secondary vertical axis**

   1. In an existing chart with more than one data series, double-click the data series you want to plot on a secondary axis.

   2. On the **Series Options** subpane of the **Format Data Series** pane, select **Secondary Axis**.

> ➤ **To change the chart type for the secondary axis**

   1. Right-click the data series, and then click **Change Series Chart Type**.

   2. In the **Change Chart Type** dialog box, in the **Choose the chart type and axis for your data series** area at the bottom of the dialog box, select the chart type you want to use for each data series.

Creating custom chart templates

Your chart formatting and customizations can be saved as a chart template that you can use to apply similar formatting to other charts. When you use the Save As Template command, a dialog box opens to the location specified for Office templates in your user profile which is, by default, the C:\Users*user name*\AppData\Roaming\Microsoft\Templates\Charts folder.

Templates that you save in this folder appear in the Templates folder in both the Insert Chart and Change Chart Type dialog boxes so that you can select the template when you create or update a chart.

> **Tip** You can also open the Insert Chart dialog box by clicking the Charts dialog box launcher.

➤ **To save a chart as a template**

1. Right-click the chart you want to save as a template, and then click **Save As Template**.

2. In the **File name** box, enter an appropriate name.

➤ **To apply a chart template**

1. Select the data you want to plot in the chart.

2. On the **Insert** tab, click any chart type in the **Charts** group, and then click **More Charts**.

3. In the **Insert Chart** dialog box, on the **Templates** page of the **All Charts** tab, click the template you want to use.

➤ **To apply a chart template to an existing chart**

1. Select the chart.

2. On the **Design** tool tab, in the **Type** group, click the **Change Chart Type** button.

3. In the **Change Chart Type** dialog box, on the **All Charts** page, select the template you want to use.

➤ **To remove or delete a chart template**

1. On the **Insert** tab, in the **Charts** group, click any chart type, and then click **More Charts**.

2. In the **Insert Chart** dialog box, click **Manage Templates** on the **All Charts** page.

3. Select a template and then move it or delete it.

> **Strategy** The Objective Domain for this test specifies "viewing chart animations" as a topic in this section. See the sidebar "Viewing chart animations," in section 4.3, "Create and manage PivotCharts."

Practice tasks

The practice file for these tasks is located in the MOSExcel2013Expert\Objective4 practice file folder. Save the results of the tasks in the same folder.

Open the *ExcelExpert_4-1* workbook and try performing the following tasks:

- Add a trendline.
- Make Yvette Kirwan's data series a secondary axis with a different chart type.
- Add another data series on the secondary axis.
- Save the chart as a template.

4.2 Create and manage PivotTables

Arranging a large data set as a PivotTable report can help facilitate your analysis and presentation of the information it contains. In a PivotTable, you can apply filters, summarize and outline data, and quickly change how the data is organized to gain additional perspective.

This section describes how to set up and work with a PivotTable and how to filter and organize data by applying a slicer.

Creating PivotTables

You can apply PivotTables to almost any kind of tabular data, but their real value comes through when working with data that can be categorized in more than one way, such as sales records that include columns for date, salesperson, and division.

The PivotTable and Recommended PivotTables commands appear in the Tables group on the Insert tab. To begin, click anywhere in the table that contains the data you want to include, and then click Recommended PivotTables.

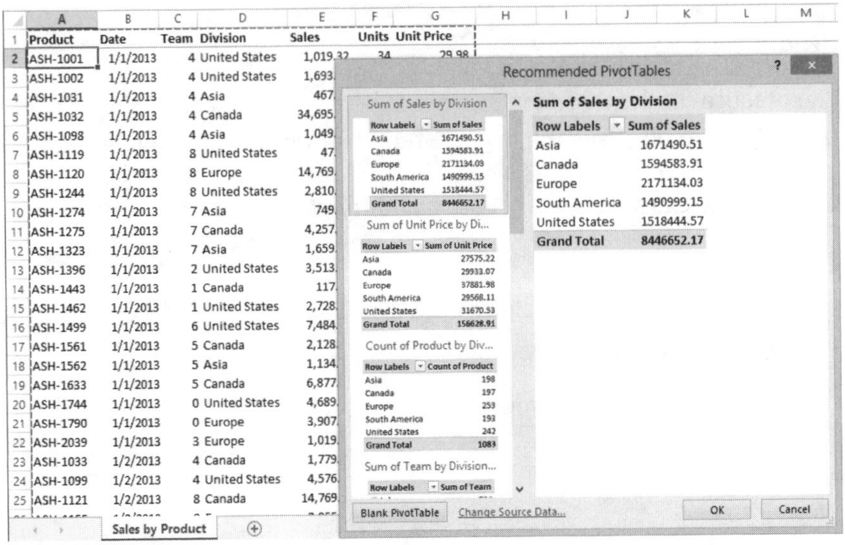

The list of Recommended PivotTables includes a selection of different table arrangements, based on the data derived from the selected table. When you select a thumbnail from the list on the left, a preview is shown on the right. If you need to select a different cell range than the one offered, click Change Source Data. Even if the suggestions are not exactly what you want, select one as a starting place and then modify it to suit your needs.

> **Tip** If you want to place a PivotTable on an existing worksheet with other data (not recommended), use the PivotTable command rather than the Recommended PivotTable command.

The PivotTable Fields pane and the PivotTable Tools tabs appear after the PivotTable is inserted, and when it is selected. The PivotTable Field list includes the column (field) headings for the data, in addition to four areas to which you add fields as you build the PivotTable. The field list offers check boxes; the currently active fields are selected. When you select a check box, Excel determines an appropriate place and inserts the field data there. If you'd rather control where you want it to go, you can drag fields between and among the field list and the areas below it. Feel free to experiment. You can always delete the worksheet and start over. Notice that when you drag a field, a gray I-beam pointer appears, showing you where the field will be inserted, which makes a difference as to where the data appears in the PivotTable.

You can change the way a field is presented by clicking the small black arrow in the field box, and click Value Field Settings (or just Field Settings) from the shortcut menu to open a dialog box of the same name.

> **Tip** You can also open the Field Settings dialog box by selecting a cell in the field you want to edit and then clicking the Field Settings button in the Active Field group on the Analyze tool tab.

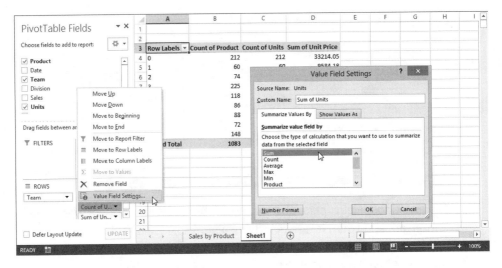

You can also use the options in the Field Settings dialog box to control additional settings, including:

- Other methods of evaluating the field. Besides Count and Sum, you can select Max, Min, Average, Product, two types each of Variance and Standard Deviation, and Count Nums, which ignores blanks.

- Changing the field name by using the Custom Name box. Change the generic names applied by Excel; for example, change *Sum of Units* to *Unit Sales*.

- Specifying a number format to be applied to the field. Applying formatting this way, as a field setting, is more reliable than formatting the PivotTable directly, which can have unexpected results after the table is filtered or pivoted.

- Applying custom calculations to each item in the values area, by using options on the Show Values As page of the dialog box, for example, % Of Grand Total, % Of Parent Row Total, % Of Parent Column Total, and Rank Smallest To Largest.

> **Tip** The dialog box that opens when you select the Field Settings command from the menu of a Rows or Columns field includes settings for layout and subtotals.

With the initial layout of the PivotTable established and the data in place, you can work with the commands on the PivotTable Tools tabs to refine it. On the Design tool tab, the PivotTable Styles gallery offers appearance options, and you can display or hide row or column headers, banded rows and columns, subtotals, and grand totals.

➤ **To create a PivotTable on a new sheet**

1. Select any cell in a table of data.

2. On the **Insert** tab, in the **Tables** group, click **Recommended PivotTables**.

3. Select a table from the suggested types, and then click **OK**.

➤ **To create a PivotTable on the current sheet**

1. Select any cell in a table of data.

2. On the **Insert** tab, in the **Tables** group, click **PivotTable**.

3. In the **Create PivotTable** dialog box, click **Existing Worksheet**, specify a location, and then click **OK**.

➤ **To modify field settings**

1. In the **PivotTable Fields** pane, click the black menu arrow in the field you want to edit, and then click **Value Field Settings** (or **Field Settings** in a **Rows** or **Columns** field).

2. Make modifications in the **Field Settings** dialog box.

Formatting PivotTables

PivotTables are dynamic. The number of rows and columns often changes drastically as you try different combinations. For this reason, it is best not to apply formatting directly to the table by clicking buttons on the Home tab. Instead, the Design tool tab contains a gallery of styles that you can use to safely apply PivotTable formatting. Preview a style on the worksheet by pointing to the thumbnail in the gallery. Click Clear at the bottom of the gallery to remove all formatting, and then you can begin again or work with a plain, unformatted PivotTable.

In the Layout group on the Design tool tab, you can select the report layout and decide whether to display blank rows between items in the PivotTable. You can choose from three standard report layouts: compact, outline, and tabular. The compact format places detail items under a row heading in the same column. In the outline format, these detail items appear in their own column, which expands the area of the PivotTable. The tabular format is similar to the outline format and displays gridlines at the borders of columns and rows.

In the PivotTable Styles group on the on the Design tool tab, you can turn row and column headings on or off, and apply banded formatting to rows and columns.

➤ **To format a PivotTable**

→ On the **Design** tool tab, select options in the **Layout** group. Then select a style from the **PivotTable Styles** gallery.

Modifying field selections and options

The Analyze tool tab offers tools for filtering, refreshing, and applying calculations to data, choosing a different data source, or selecting a different PivotTable type, among other tasks. You can also choose filtering options that are available on the row or column header menus that appear in a PivotTable.

Using field headers

The field headers (row labels and/or column labels) contain arrow buttons that display a menu offering tools that you can use to sort and filter the data in the table.

There are commands for sorting and filtering data based on the values (Value Filters) and/or the labels (Label Filters). You can use the search box to locate an item, which is helpful in a long list. Select the check boxes in the list of items under the search box to select individual values (categories) to include. For example, to filter for specific categories, select the Select All check box to clear it, and then select the check boxes for each category you want. You can clear filters by clicking the Clear Filter From *field name* command, which appears on the filter menu whenever the funnel icon is visible.

	A	B	C	D	E
1	Sales by Team				
2					
3	Team	Product Lines	Unit Sales	Team Sales	
4	1	60	3,021	$9,584	
5	2	74	6,253	$7,791	
6	7	72	4,158	$5,311	
7	Grand Total	206	13,432	$22,686	
8					
9					

Changing your view of the data

In addition to applying filters with field headers, you can manipulate your PivotTable to change the way the data is summarized and presented. You can even add or remove data. With the PivotTable Field pane visible, you can drag fields in the Filters, Columns, Rows, and Values areas to other locations, or drag them outside the list to remove them. (You can always drag fields back down from the field list again if you change your mind.)

> **Tip** If it is not already visible, you can display the PivotTable Field pane by clicking Field List on the Show menu on the Analyze tool tab.

PivotTable Fields ▾ ✕

Choose fields to add to report: ⚙ ▾

- ☑ Product
- ☐ Date
- ☑ Team
- ☑ Division
- ☐ Sales
- ☐ Units

Drag fields between areas below:

▼ FILTERS

▥ COLUMNS
Team ▾

▦ ROWS
Division ▾

Σ VALUES
Product Lines ▾

☐ Defer Layout Update   UPDATE

	A	B	C	D	E	F	G	H	I	J	K	L
1	Product Lines by Division											
2												
3	Product Lines	Team ▾										
4	Division ▾		0	1	2	3	4	5	6	7	8 Grand Total	
5	Asia		42	11	11	42	27	13	15	17	20	198
6	Canada		38	10	13	39	24	17	16	10	30	197
7	Europe		46	15	16	51	27	18	21	25	34	253
8	South America		42	7	16	43	13	20	16	9	27	193
9	United States		44	17	18	50	27	18	20	11	37	242
10	Grand Total		212	60	74	225	118	86	88	72	148	1,083
11												
12												
13												
14												
15												
16												
17												
18												
19												
20												
21												

◀ ▶ ... Sheet1 **PivotTable2** ⊕

READY

Using calculated fields and items

A *calculated field* is a new field that is derived from calculations performed on other fields. Inserting a calculated field adds a new column. A *calculated item* is a new item that is derived from calculations performed on other items in the same field. Inserting a calculated item adds a new row. Each cell in the new row or column contains the formula entered in the dialog box. To define a calculated field or item, select Fields, Items, and Sets from the Calculations menu.

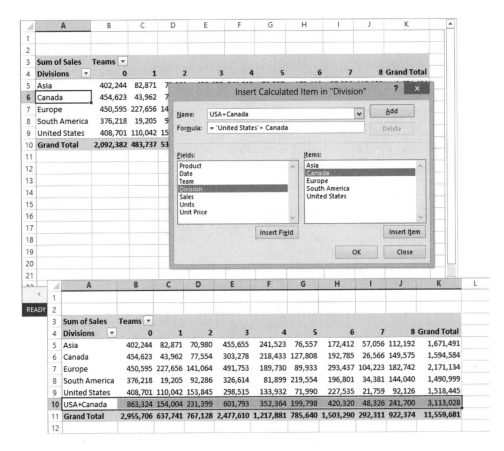

Tip If you need to edit the formula for a calculated item or field, open the appropriate dialog box, select the item or field you want in the Name list, and then click Modify or Delete.

➤ **To create a calculated field in a PivotTable**

1. Select any cell in the PivotTable.

2. On the **Analyze** tool tab, in the **Calculations** group, click the **Fields, Items, & Sets** button, and then click **Calculated Field**.

3. Name your field in the **Name** box.

4. Edit the sample formula by using operators and inserting available fields by clicking the **Insert Field** button.

➤ **To create a calculated item in a PivotTable**

1. Select any cell in the row or column headings of the PivotTable.

2. On the **Analyze** tool tab, in the **Calculations** group, click the **Fields, Items, & Sets** button, and then click **Calculated Item**.

3. Name your field in the **Name** box.

4. Edit the sample formula by using operators and inserting available fields and items by clicking the **Insert Field** or **Insert Item** button.

Creating slicers

Slicers are handy tools you can use to interactively filter PivotTables. In the Insert Slicers dialog box, which you open by clicking the Insert Slicer button in the Filter group on the Analyze tool tab, select the field or fields for which you want to create a slicer. Excel creates the slicer as an object with controls you use to select "slices" of data, such as sales of a specific division, over a specific period of time, from a specific team. You can apply multiple slicers to a PivotTable (or a regular table), and you can use them all at the same time.

You work with slicers by using commands on the Options tool tab, which appears on the ribbon when you select a slicer. Use the Slicer Styles gallery to apply formatting to a slicer. (Styles change the fill color and shading of selected and unselected items in a slicer.) Use controls in the Arrange, Buttons, and Size groups to align, group, and resize slicers just as you can with any other object.

> **Tip** You can assign a macro that runs when you click a slicer. Right-click the slicer, and then choose Assign Macro. Click Record to start recording the macro, or click New to write the macro's code yourself in the Microsoft Visual Basic Editor.

In the Slicer Settings dialog box, which you open from the Slicer group or by right-clicking a slicer, you can rename the slicer, change the caption, and set options for how the items in the slicer are sorted and filtered.

To create a slicer

1. On the **Analyze** tool tab, click **Insert Slicer**.
2. Select the field or fields for which you want to create slicers.

To apply a slicer

→ Click a slicer button, or drag through a series of buttons, or hold down the **Ctrl** key and click to select non-adjacent filter buttons.

To clear a slicer

→ Click the filter (funnel) button in the upper-right corner of the slicer box.

➤ **To modify a slicer**

→ Right-click the slicer, and then click **Slicer Settings**.

Using PowerPivot

PowerPivot, first introduced in Excel 2010, is an add-in you can use to create sophisticated data models by building relationships among multiple tables. Much of the underlying infrastructure of the PowerPivot add-in is now built into Excel, including the Excel Data Model, which you can use to import massive amounts of data, create relationships between data from different sources, address multiple tables, and manage data connections.

PowerPivot is a COM add-in, so you need to install it from the Add-ins page of the Excel Options dialog box. When you do, a new PowerPivot tab appears on the ribbon.

Here are some of the tasks you can perform by using PowerPivot:

- Create your own hierarchies.
- Define key performance indicators (KPIs).
- Create *perspectives* (customizable views of PowerPivot data).
- Use advanced data-management and modeling tools.
- Manage relationships by dragging.
- Perform calculations by using special Data Analysis Expression (DAX) language functions.
- Filter data and rename tables while importing.
- Create PivotTables and PivotCharts.
- Save PowerPivot workbooks to Microsoft SharePoint for enhanced functionality and collaboration by using PowerPivot for SharePoint 2013.

> **Tip** As of this writing, the PowerPivot and Power View features are included only with specific configurations of Office 2013. The PowerPivot feature, which was available in all versions of Excel 2010, is available only in Office 2013 Professional Plus, SharePoint 2013 Enterprise Edition, SharePoint Online 2013 Plan 2, and the E3 or E4 editions of Office 365. The Power View feature, new in Excel 2013, is included with the same editions as PowerPivot. The Excel Data Model is supported in all editions of Excel. These policies might change, so if the PowerPivot add-in is available for you to install, you're good to go.

You can open PowerPivot after loading data into Excel, or you can load data directly into the PowerPivot window by using the Get External Data button. In either case, PowerPivot requires data to be in the data model. You can add data to the data model when you import. If you import a multitable database file, data is automatically added to the data model. Otherwise, you can choose to add it when you import by using the options in the Import Data dialog box.

> **Tip** The advantages of importing data through the PowerPivot program's Get External Data menu are that you can filter out unnecessary data and rename tables and columns before you import data into the data model, eliminating the need to store unnecessary data.

Tables that you import into the data model become separate tabs in the PowerPivot window. It is important to note that data contained in the data model is separate from data on worksheets. Even if you load data into the data model from worksheet tables, the data is pulled into the data model and exists outside the worksheet. The data model is what you might call a "virtual data cube."

> **Important** Tables need to have relationships with one another to be useful in a multi-table model, which essentially means having columns of data in common. For more information, see the "Managing relationships" topic later in this section.

On the PowerPivot tab, click the Manage button—the only item in the Data Model group—to open PowerPivot in a separate window. When you do, Excel displays the tables, fields, and records of the current data model in PowerPivot. Fields and records are visible in tables, each of which has its own tab across the bottom of the window.

You can add existing worksheet data to the data model by clicking the Add To Data Model button on the PowerPivot tab. When you use this method, it is highly advisable to create separate Excel tables (preferably on separate worksheets) for each table you want to add, using the Table button on the Insert tab, making sure to specify the My Table Has Headers option. The names you give to each table become the tab names of the tables as shown in the PowerPivot window, which become linked to the worksheet tables when you add them to the data model. Once linked, any edits made to the worksheet tables will update the corresponding tabs in the PowerPivot window automatically, but once updated, the data model no longer uses the worksheet tables.

➤ **To install the PowerPivot add-in**

1. In the **Backstage** view, click **Options**.

2. In the **Excel Options** dialog box, on the **Add-Ins** page, in the **Manage** list, select **COM Add-ins**, and then click **Go**.

3. Select **Microsoft Office PowerPivot for Excel 2013**, and then click **OK**.

➤ **To launch PowerPivot**

→ On the **PowerPivot** tab, click **Manage**.

➤ **To import data into the data model**

1. On the **Data** tab, click **Get External Data**, and select an option. (Not all options allow access to the data model.)

2. Select a data source, and any other necessary options.

3. In the **Import Data** dialog box, along with any other necessary options, click **Add this data to the data model**.

➤ **To add data from tables to the data model**

1. Select a cell anywhere in an Excel table.

2. On the **PowerPivot** tab, click **Add to Data Model**.

Managing relationships

You might have already created a relationship. If you add a second table to a PivotTable, create a Power View report, or click the Relationships button on the Data tab to create a relationship between tables in a workbook, a data model is created. In fact, the presence of a relationship is what distinguishes a data model from just a bunch of tables.

A *relationship* is a connection based on the existence of a common column of data in two tables; that is, data that means the same thing in both tables, even if the columns have different names.

If you import data from a relational database file, chances are that relationships already exist. Excel recognizes most relationships when you import data, and uses them to create a data model on the fly. If you import data from flat files, text files, or worksheet tables, you will need to create relationships yourself. After creating relationships, PowerPivot can retrieve columns of data from any related table.

The important things to remember when creating relationships are:

- Each table must have a column in common with another table, containing equivalent data.

- For each pair of connected tables, one of the common columns must contain only unique entries, no duplicate values.

In the Create Relationship dialog box, you need to specify the table name and column name for each pair of connected tables. The lists in the dialog box represent all the tables in the data model and the fields they contain.

- **Table** The source table that contains the values you want to match

- **Column** The source table column that contains the values you're matching (also known as the Foreign key column)

⊠ **Related table** The table that contains the values you want to find

⊠ **Related lookup column** The column in the related table that contains the values matching the foreign key column

For example, you could create a relationship between a large table of sales detail data and another table that lists sales teams, using team numbers as the common column. In the sales table, each team number appears many times; in the teams table, each number appears just once.

After you create relationships, you can access fields from all connected tables in your analysis. For example, if you click the PivotTable button on the Home tab of the PowerPivot window after creating relationships, both tables are listed in the PivotTable Field pane. Addressing multiple tables like this is only possible when using the data model.

In the following screen shot, the Sales by Product table supplies the Division and Sum of Sales data, and the Teams table supplies the team names displayed under Row Labels. The team names do not exist in the SalesByProduct table—only team numbers—but because a relationship is created by using the common Team column, you can use data from both tables as if they were one.

> ➤ **To create a relationship between tables**

1. Open a workbook that contains at least two tables that have a common column.

2. On the **Data** tab, in the **Data Tools** group, click **Relationships**.

3. In the **Relationships** dialog box, click **New**.

4. In the **Create Relationship** dialog box, select the source table and column, and the related table and column from the lists.

> ➤ **To edit a relationship**

1. Open a workbook that contains a relationship (data model).

2. On the **Data** tab, in the **Data Tools** group, click **Relationships**.

3. In the **Manage Relationships** dialog box, select the relationship you want to modify, and then click **Edit**.

4. In the **Edit Relationship** dialog box, make your changes.

➤ **To activate, deactivate, or delete a relationship**

1. Open a workbook that contains a relationship (data model).

2. On the **Data** tab, in the **Data Tools** group, click **Relationships**.

3. In the **Manage Relationships** dialog box, select the relationship you want to modify, and then click **Activate**, **Deactivate**, or **Delete**.

Creating hierarchies

A *hierarchy* in PowerPivot is literally a group of columns that appear as a single item, representing different levels for similar data. For example, you can create common hierarchies such as city/state/country, or employee/supervisor/manager to allow you to use a single field to drill down (or up) for different levels of detail.

Excel initially bases hierarchies on the *cardinality* of the data contained in the specified columns; that is, the relative uniqueness of the values. Higher cardinalities, where the values in the column are the most unique, are listed first (for example, Country). Lower cardinalities, where the values in the column are the least unique are listed last (for example, City).

Hierarchies are defined as parent/child levels, where the parent level is the column with higher cardinality, and the child level is the column with lower cardinality. Excel is pretty good at figuring all this out, but you can make modifications.

Here are some things you can and can't do with hierarchies:

- You can add columns to a hierarchy by dragging in Diagram view.
- You can change the parent/child levels by dragging an item to another level.
- You can rename a hierarchy or any of the child levels.
- You can hide the names of the source columns.
- You can add a column to only one hierarchy at a time.

To create a hierarchy, you need to be in Diagram view in PowerPivot, where you select the columns you want before clicking Create Hierarchy. Doing so creates a new Hierarchy item in the table containing subordinate items that match the columns you originally selected, with the source column name in parentheses. You can change the names of the subordinate items and hide the source column names, if you want.

When you create a PivotTable, the hierarchy appears as an item in the Fields list, and just like other fields, you can drag it to one of the areas at the bottom of the Fields list to apply it to the PivotTable.

Sum of Sales	Column Labels						
Row Labels	Blue	Cyan	Gold	Green	Magenta	Orange	Purple
⊞ Asia	70980.32	76556.72	112192.29	82871.04	241522.91	172412.23	57055.72
⊟ Canada	77554.27	127807.96	149574.51	43962.37	218432.57	192784.56	26566.32
AL		30357.58	12387.62			615.7	6188
BC	6308.44	11458.76	8721.8	36202.87	31266.64	45132.64	
BD	39857.24	411.22	3806.3		5630.94	18854.4	
MA				565.8	24566.61	18841.62	14684
NB	1018.44	15318.38	2777.44		41130.1		
NF	943						
NS	14787		31216.78	565.8	39306.97		4420.9
ON	1838.85	54306.88	32245.1	4.7	15992.88	53073.72	858.5
QU	1037.3	15955.14	5088.45	117.5	25842.93	13911.59	
SA	11764		53331.02	6505.7	34695.7	42354.89	414.92
⊞ Europe	141064.2	89933.22	182742.06	227656.31	189729.9	293436.95	104223.07
⊞ South America	92285.83	219554.37	144039.99	19205.15	81899.18	196800.72	34381.11
⊞ United States	153844.61	71990.08	92125.55	110041.81	133931.77	227535.35	21759.34
Grand Total	535729.23	585842.35	680674.4	483736.68	865516.33	1082969.81	243985.56

PivotTable Fields

ACTIVE   ALL

Choose fields to add to report:

▲ ▦ SalesByProduct
  ▷ ☑ **Division Hierarchy**
  ▷ ▦ More Fields
▲ ▦ Teams
  ☐ Last Name
  ☐ First Name
  ☐ Title

Drag fields between areas below:

▼ FILTERS	▦ COLUMNS
	Team Name ▼

▦ ROWS	Σ VALUES
Division Hier... ▼	Sum of Sales ▼

☐ Defer Layout Update   UPDATE

| Sales | Sheet1 | Teams | ⊕ |

➤ To create a hierarchy

1. On the **Home** tab of the PowerPivot window, click **Diagram View**.

2. Select the fields you want to use (hold down **Shift** and then click to select adjacent fields or hold down **Ctrl** and then click to select nonadjacent fields).

3. Right-click one of the selected fields, and then click **Create Hierarchy**.

4. Enter a name for the hierarchy.

➤ To rename a hierarchy or child level

➔ Right-click the item, and then click **Rename**.

➤ **To edit a hierarchy**

→ Right-click the field or hierarchy you want to edit, and then select a command (**Hide Source Column Name**, **Move Up**, **Move Down**, **Remove from Hierarchy** or **Rename**).

→ Drag a field to move it to a new location in the hierarchy.

➤ **To delete a hierarchy**

→ Right-click the hierarchy, and then click **Delete**.

Practice tasks

The practice files for these tasks are located in the MOSExcel2013Expert\Objective4 practice file folder. Save the results of the tasks in the same folder.

▣ Open the *ExcelExpert_4-2a* workbook and try performing the following tasks:

    ▣ Create a PivotTable by using the data it contains.

    ▣ On Sheet1, use the options in the Value Field Settings dialog box to apply number formatting and edit the field names.

▣ Open the *ExcelExpert_4-2b* workbook and try performing the following tasks:

    ▣ Add the table on each tab to the data model.

    ▣ From the PowerPivot program window, create a PivotTable.

4.3 Create and manage PivotCharts

PivotCharts are a graphical tool that you can create to accompany a PivotTable. You work with PivotCharts in many of the same ways you work with PivotTables. You should review section 4.2, "Create and manage PivotTables," to learn how to work with data in a PivotTable.

Creating PivotCharts

The Create PivotChart dialog box opens when you click the PivotChart button in the Charts group on the Insert tab. In this dialog box, you specify the cell range that contains the data you are working with or click Use An External Data Source to set up data from a source outside the workbook. If the active cell is in a table, Excel selects the table. You can choose whether to add the PivotChart to a new worksheet or to a location on the current worksheet, and whether to add the selection to the data model.

After Excel creates the placeholders for the PivotTable and the PivotChart, use the PivotTable Field list to drag the fields you want to use to the areas of the PivotChart: Filters, Legend (Series), Axis (Categories), and Values. If you select the field's check box, Excel adds it to the area it determines is appropriate. (A field with numbers is added to the Values area, for example.) You can modify the organization of the chart by moving fields to different areas—by dragging the fields or by right-clicking the field and using commands on the shortcut menu.

> **Tip** You can insert an associated PivotChart after you create a PivotTable by clicking PivotChart in the Tools group on the Options tool tab.

After you build the initial PivotChart, you work with the data it presents by using the PivotChart Tools tabs:

- **Analyze** Use the options in the Active Field group to show or hide details for the field. From the Filter group, you can insert a slicer or a timeline, and apply filters to data connections. In the Data group, you can refresh the data or change the data source. Use the options in the Show/Hide group to control whether the PivotTable Field list and field buttons are displayed.

- **Design** Use the options on the Design tool tab to change the chart type, switch the row and column orientation, modify the data range for the chart, and apply a layout and style.

- **Format** Use the Format Selection command to open the appropriate formatting dialog box or pane. On the Format tool tab, you can also apply shape styles (to the columns in a column chart, for example) and text effects, and specify dimensions for a chart. You use the options in the Insert Shapes group to add graphic elements, and the options in the Arrange group to help locate, align, group, and ungroup shapes.

> **See Also** For more information about working with charts, see section 4.1, "Create advanced chart elements."

Viewing chart animations

In Excel 2013, everything is animated. You'll notice this whenever you insert or delete rows or columns. When you do, the rows or columns to the right or below slide into place with a hint of movement in the appropriate direction. Chart animations are a bit more dramatic, which will be obvious when manipulating a PivotChart. When you change the underlying data, the chart doesn't change immediately, but takes a second to "morph" into a new shape. Very nice.

Manipulating options in existing PivotCharts

Keep in mind that the data and view for a PivotChart depends in part on how you organize and change the PivotTable the chart is based on. For example, when you apply a filter to the PivotTable, that filter also affects the data displayed in the PivotChart. The same holds true when you filter the data shown in the PivotChart. A filter you apply to the chart changes the display of the PivotTable.

To show or hide the PivotTable Field list and the field buttons on the chart, use the commands in the Show/Hide group on the Analyze tool tab. You should display the field list when you want to reposition fields or to add or remove a field from the PivotChart (and PivotTable). For example, you can switch the axis and the legend fields or combine fields in these areas to alter the data in the chart.

Use the field buttons in a PivotChart as you do the field headers in a PivotTable to apply a filter directly to the chart. You can use the menu that is displayed to sort the data in the chart, to apply a label or a value filter, to search for a specific item, or to select a subset of the data.

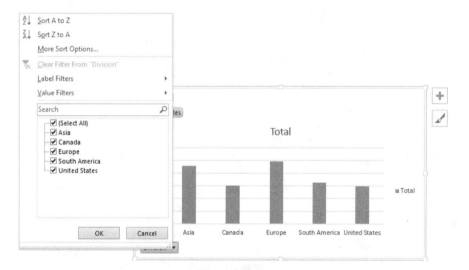

To analyze the data in a PivotChart in other ways, select the PivotTable that's associated with the PivotChart and then use the commands on the Analyze and Design tool tabs.

➤ **To create a PivotChart**

1. On the **Insert** tab, in the **Charts** group, click **PivotChart**, or click the PivotChart arrow and then click **Pivot Chart & PivotTable** to create both at once.

2. In the **Create PivotChart** dialog box, specify the data range to use or click the option to use an external data source.

3. Choose the option to place the PivotChart on a new worksheet or in a location on the current worksheet. Then click **OK**.

4. In the **PivotTable Field** list, drag the fields to the areas where you want them to appear in the chart: **Filters**, **Legend (Series)**, **Axis (Categories)**, or **Values**.

➤ **To rearrange a PivotChart and sort and filter data**

1. To change the view of the data in a PivotChart, use the **PivotTable Field** list to place a field in a different area or to combine fields.

2. To sort the data shown in a PivotChart, click the arrow beside a field button and then choose a sort option.

3. To filter the data shown in a PivotChart, click the arrow beside a field button and then define a label filter or a value filter or select the check boxes to select a subset of the data.

Applying styles to PivotCharts

You can apply styles to a PivotChart just like you can with regular charts: by using the options in the Chart Styles group on the Design tool tab. Point to a style in the Chart Styles gallery to see a live preview of the style displayed on the chart. Click the style thumbnail to apply it. If you click the Change Color button, the color gallery used in all the displayed chart styles changes accordingly.

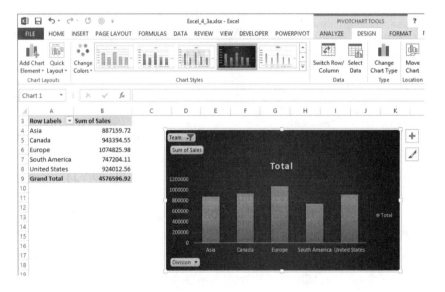

➤ **To apply a style to a PivotChart**

→ Select the PivotChart, and then in the **Chart Styles** gallery on the **Design** tool tab, point to any thumbnail to preview the style. Click the thumbnail to apply it to the chart.

➤ **To change the color palette of displayed styles**

→ Click the **Change Colors** button, and then select a palette.

Practice tasks

The practice file for these tasks is located in the MOSExcel2013Expert\Objective4 practice file folder. Save the results of the tasks in the same folder.

Open the *ExcelExpert_4-3* workbook and try performing the following tasks:

- Create a PivotChart showing sales by Division.
- Create a slicer for Teams.
- Select a style for the chart and modify the color scheme.

Objective review

Before finishing this chapter, ensure that you have mastered the following skills:

4.1 Create advanced chart elements
4.2 Create and manage PivotTables
4.3 Create and manage PivotCharts

Index

Symbols and numbers

" " (quotation marks), in logical tests 88
(number sign), in format codes for numbers 43
#DIV/0! 35
#N/A 35
#NAME? 35
#NULL! 36
#NUM! 36
#REF! 35
#VALUE 35
% (percent sign), in format codes for numbers 43
& (ampersand), concatenating with 103
* (asterisk), in format codes for numbers 44
, (thousands separator), in format codes for numbers 44
. (decimal point) 43
.csv files, passwords and 27
= (equal sign), in logical tests 88
? (question mark), in format codes for numbers 43
@ (at symbol), in format codes for numbers 44
\ (backslash), in format codes for numbers 44
_ (underscore), in format codes for numbers 44
0 (zero), in format codes for numbers 43

A

accepting changes 31
Access, importing data from 11, 13
Accessibility Checker 76–78
accessibility, preparing workbooks for 76
accounting number formats
    creating custom 47
    dollar signs in 46
    syntax for 45
ACCRINT function 93
ACCRINTM function 93
activating
    relationships 145
    sheet protection 19
add-ins, Solver 110
aligning dollar signs 46
aligning numbers by using formatting characters 44–45
alt text (alternative text) 77–78

amortization
    calculating 91
    time-based calculations and 101
AM/PM, codes for formatting 50
ampersand (&), concatenating with 103
AND function 87
animations, in PivotCharts 150
arguments
    col_index_num 96
    criteria_range 89
    defined 86
    for investment functions 91
    lookup_value 96
    lookup_vector 98
    range_lookup 96
    result_vector 98
    return_type 103
    row_index_num 96
    securities analysis 94
    serial_number 103
    sum_range 89
    table_array 96
    value_if_false 88
    value_if_true 88
    weekend 104
array formulas 99–100
asterisk (*), in format codes for numbers 44
at symbol (@), in format codes for numbers 44
auditing formulas 39
AutoCorrect options 80
AutoFill capabilities 53
AutoRecover 6–7
AVERAGEIF function
    purpose 89
    syntax 88
AVERAGEIFS function
    purpose 89
    syntax 88
axis, secondary value 123

B

backslash (\), in format codes for numbers 44
bar charts, conditional formatting for 55
blank cells, accessibility and 78

body style, fonts for 83
breaking external references 15
buttons, inserting 73

C

calculated fields and items 136–137
calculating
  depreciation 92–93
  investments 90
  loan payments 91
calculations
  checking for errors 36
  current workbook 27
  current worksheet 27
  described 25
  iterative 26–27, 107
  options 25, 27
  subordinate, in nested functions 87
captioning, accessibility and 78
cardinality, hierarchies and 145
categories of metadata 24
cell ranges
  constraints and 109
  naming 106, 108
cell styles
  colors 66
  creating 66
  custom 7
  described 65
  modifying 66
cells
  constraints and 109
  naming 106, 108
change history log 17–18
change tracking
  accepting revisions 31
  described 16
  displaying all 31
  exclusions 17
  history log 17–18
  options 16, 18
  passwords and 17
  rejecting revisions 31
  reviewing changes 31
  scope 17
  sharing and 17
  tables and 17
  turning off 19
  turning on 18
charts
  bar, conditional formatting for 55
  described 119

  drop lines 122
  high-low lines 122
  secondary axis 123
  templates for 127–128
  trendlines 120–122
  type, changing for secondary axis 126
  up-down bars 122
check box form control 71, 74–75
checking accessibility features 76, 78
checking spelling, in other languages 81
circular references 26, 107
clearing conditional formatting rules 62
codes. *See* format codes
color scales 56
color schemes
  PivotCharts and 153
  templates and 66
color sets
  custom 67–68
  managing multiple 83
columns 142
combo box form control 71, 74
command button form control 71, 75
comments 32
CONCATENATE function 103
concatenating text in formulas 103
conditional formatting
  applying 58
  applying multiple on same cells 60
  clearing all rules 62
  color scales 56
  custom 56, 58
  data bars 55, 57–58
  described 55
  editing rules 62
  formulas 58–59
  highlight cells 55–56
  icon sets 56
  managing rules 61–62
  PivotTables options 60
  rule categories 55
  rule types 57
  top/bottom 55–56
conditional tests. *See* logical functions
configuring change tracking options 18
connecting tables 142
connections, data. *See* importing data
consolidating data. *See* data, consolidating
constraints, in Solver models 107, 109
controls, adding alt text to 78
copying
  macros 9
  styles 7, 9

corresponding field, scoping by 60
COUNTIF function
    purpose 89
    syntax 88
COUNTIFS function
    purpose 89
    syntax 88
COUPDAYBS function 94
COUPDAYS function 94
COUPDAYSNC function 94
COUPNCD function 94
COUPNUM function 94
coupons, bonds and 95
COUPPCD function 94
.csv files, passwords and 27
custom
    cell styles 66
    chart templates 127
    color sets 67–68
    conditional formats 56, 58
    date formats 47–49
    fill sequence 53–54
    font sets 67–68
    number formats 42, 47
    styles, copying between templates 7
    templates 63–64
    themes 69
    time formats 49–51

D

data bars
    conditional formatting 55
    negative values in 57
    options 58
Data Connection Wizard 12
data connections. *See* importing data
data, consolidating
    adding sheets 115
    by category 113, 115–117
    described 113
    dynamic 116
    by position 113–116
    rerunning 116
data mining. *See* lookup functions
data models
    cell styles and 65
    importing data 140, 142
    PowerPivot and 139
    vs. tables 142
    tables, adding to 141–142

    as virtual data cubes 140
    what-if analysis and 106
data series, adding multiple to the same chart 125
date formats, custom 47–49
dates
    functions for calculating. *See* functions
    holidays, including in calculations 104
    how Excel calculates 47, 100
    weekends, including in calculations 104
DATEVALUE function 102, 105
DAY function 102
days of the week, functions and 103
DB function 92
DDB function 92
deactivating relationships 145
decimal point (.) 43
declining balance depreciation 92–93
deductions, calculating depreciation for 92
default storage location for templates 5
deleting
    chart templates 128
    custom formats 47
    hierarchies 148
    relationships 145
    scenarios 113
    trendlines 123
dependent cells, viewing 87
dependents, tracing 38–39
depreciation 92–93
Developer tab, displaying 9
digits, controlling number of on each side of
        decimal point 43
DISC function 94
display language 80
displaying
    all tracked changes 31
    change tracking 30
    comments 32
    data in international formats 79
    Developer tab 9
    formulas 38
    on-screen keyboard 83
    startup prompt when updating external
        references 15
distributing copies 33–34
#DIV/0! 35
Document Inspector 24
dollar signs, aligning 46
DOLLARDE function 93
DOLLARFR function 93
drop lines 122
dual-axis charts. *See* secondary axis charts
DURATION function 94

E

editing
   changing language for 80
   conditional formatting 62
   formatting rules 57–59, 61
   formula links 12
   functions 86
   hierarchies 145, 148
   relationships 144
   restrictions 19–21
   scenarios 111, 113
   themes 69–70
elapsed time format codes for 51
encrypting
   with passwords 28
   workbooks 27
equal sign (=), in logical tests 88
errors
   in calculations 36
   dependents, tracing 38–39
   in formulas 35
   manually checking for 37
   precedents, tracing 38–39
   tracing 37, 39
   turning off checking for 36–37
   values that appear in cells 35
evolutionary solving method 109
Excel Data Model 11, 139
Excel Services 10, 14
Excel Solver. *See* Solver
existing connections, importing data from 12, 14
exponential trendlines 120
exponents, format codes for 44
extending a series 51
external references 15

F

FALSE, result of logical operation 87–88
fields
   calculated 136–137
   headers 134
   PivotTable 131–132, 149
files, encrypting 28
filling a series
   linear vs. growth 52
   nonnumeric 53
   options 51
   procedure 54
filtering data 134–135
filtering PivotCharts 151–152
final, marking as 28–29

financial functions
   See also international formats
   described 90
   inserting 95
finding functions 90
font sets, custom 67–68
forecasting. *See* trendlines
foreign key 142
form controls
   check box 71, 74–75
   combo box 71, 74
   command button 71, 75
   described 70
   formatting 72
   group box 72–74
   inserting 70, 73
   label 72, 75
   list box 71, 74
   option button 71, 74–75
   scroll bar 71
   setting properties 75
   spin button 71, 74
format codes
   for dates 47–49
   for numbers 42–45
formatting
   conditional. *See* conditional formatting
   form controls 72
   PivotCharts 150
   PivotTables 133–134
   slicers 138
formulas
   array 99–100
   circular references in 26
   concatenating text in 103
   conditional formatting and 58–59
   displaying 38
   errors in, identifying 35–36
   hiding 19
   inconsistent with adjacent cells 36
   links, editing 12
   manually checking for errors 37
   removing auditing arrows 39
   tracing errors 37–39
   turning off error checking 36
   viewing dependent cells 87
   viewing with watch window 110
fractions, format codes for 44
functions
   AND 87
   arguments 86, 88–89
   AVERAGEIF 88–89
   AVERAGEIFS 88
   conditional formatting and 58–59

COUNTIF 88
COUNTIFS 88–89
date and time 100–101
DATEVALUE 102, 105
DAY 102
depreciation 92
editing 86
finding 86, 90
HLOOKUP 96–97
IF 87
inserting 86, 89
investment 90
library of 85
LOOKUP 98
nested 87
NETWORKDAYS 103–104
NOW 101, 104
OR 87
securities analysis 93
SUMIF 88
SUMIFS 88
TIMEVALUE 105
TODAY 101, 104
TRANSPOSE 98
VLOOKUP 96–97
volatile 101
WEEKDAY 103
WORKDAY 103–104
WORKDAY.INTL 104
fundamental tasks in Excel, not covered in this book 1
future value function 90

G

Goal Seek command 26
  described 106
  identifying goal using 107
GRG Nonlinear solving method 109
group box form control 72–74
growth series 52

H

heading style, fonts for 83
Help, configuring language for 80
hiding formulas 19
hierarchies
  adding to PivotTables 146
  cardinality and 145
  creating 146–147
  deleting 148
  described 145

  editing 145, 148
  renaming 147
highlight cells
  conditional formatting rules 55
  modifying default formats 56
high-low lines 122
HLOOKUP function 96–97
holidays, calculating dates and 104
HOUR function 102
hours, codes for formatting 50
hyperlinks, accessibility and 78

I

icon sets, conditional formatting 56
IF function 87
IF statements, circular references and 26
images, adding alt text to 78
importing data
  from Access 11, 13
  into data model 140–141
  described 10
  Excel Data Model and 11
  existing connections 12, 14
  from other sources 12
  relationships and 142
  from SQL Server 12
  from text 11, 13
  from web 11, 13
  XML 12
inserting
  change history log as new worksheet 18
  DATEVALUE function 105
  financial functions 95
  form controls 70, 73–74
  functions 86, 89
  international symbols 83
  LOOKUP function 100
  NOW functions 104
  PivotCharts 149
  scenarios 111
  slicers 138
  TIMEVALUE function 105
  TODAY functions 104
  TRANSPOSE functions 99
inspecting workbooks 23–24, 78
installing PowerPivot 139, 141
interest, calculating accruals 95
interest payment (IPMT) function 90
interface text, changing language for 80
international formats, displaying data in 79
international symbols 82–83
internationalization, preparing workbooks for 76

INTRATE function 94
investment functions 90–91
items, calculated 136–137
iterative calculations
   described 26
   enabling 107
   setting maximum 27

K

keyboard
   changing layout language for 82
   on-screen, displaying 83

L

label form control 72, 75
language pairs 81
languages
   additional, installing 79
   changing 79, 81
   checking for installed 81
   downloading additional 81
   for editing 80
   enabling 81
   keyboard layout, changing for 82
   for proofing 80–81
   spell check for each 81
   translating 82
linear series 52
linear trendlines 120
linking formulas 12
links
   breaking 15
   updating 12, 15
list box form control 71, 74
literal character strings, format codes for 44
literal demarcation characters, format codes for 44
loan payments
   calculating 91
   time-based calculations and 101
locking worksheets 19–20
logarithmic trendlines 120
logical functions 87–88
logical operators 87–88
lookup functions
   described 96
   HLOOKUP 96
   LOOKUP 98, 100
   sorting 98
   TRANSPOSE 98–99
   VLOOKUP 96

M

macros
   copying 9–10
   described 9
   enabling 9
   recording 9
   security 9
   slicers and 138
manual
   calculations 25
   error checking 37
marking as final 28–29
Maximum Change setting 26
MDURATION function 94
merged cells, accessibility and 78
merging
   scenarios 112
   styles 8
   workbooks 33–35
metadata
   categories 24
   described 23
   vs. properties 24
   removing 76
Microsoft Query, connecting to data 12
Microsoft SharePoint, Excel Services and 10
Microsoft SQL Server, connecting to 12
Microsoft Translator 81
Microsoft Visual Basic for Applications (VBA),
      copying macros and 9
MINUTE function 102
minutes, codes for formatting 50
MONTH function 102
moving average trendlines 120
multiple tables, analyzing 11

N

#N/A 35
#NAME? 35
naming
   cells and cell ranges 106, 108
   columns, for accessibility 78
   worksheets, for accessibility 78
navigating error tracing 38
nested functions 87
net present value (NPV) function 90
NETWORKDAYS function 103–104
NETWORKDAYS.INTL function 104
nonnumeric series, filling 53
NOW function 101, 104
#NULL! 36
#NUM! 36

number sign (#), in format codes for numbers 43
numbers
  aligning 44
  customizing display of 43
numeric formatting 42–45

O

objects
  adding alt text to 78
  tab order 73
on-screen keyboard, displaying 83
option button form control 71, 74–75
OR function 87
Oracle, connecting to 12
overwriting same-named styles 8

P

passwords
  encryption and 27–28
  file formats and 27
  options 28
  protecting workbooks 20
  removing encrypting 28
Pause button, Goal Seek and 106
payment (PMT) function 90
payments for loans, calculating 91–92
percent sign (%), in format codes for numbers 43
percentages, format codes for 43
periods
  for depreciation calculations 93
  for forecasting with trendlines 122
  for loan payments 91
permissions, enabling for specified cells 21
PivotCharts
  analyzing 150–151
  animations in 150
  changing colors 153
  creating 149, 151
  Data Model and 11
  described 148
  designing 150
  filtering 151–152
  formatting 150
  inserting 149
  PivotTables and 149–150
  rearranging 149, 152
  sorting 152
  styles, applying to 152–153
PivotTables
  calculated fields and items 136–137

compact format 133
  conditional formats and 60
  creating 143
  Data Model and 11
  described 129
  field headers 134
  field list 131, 135, 149
  field settings 132–133
  filters, applying 134
  formatting 133–134
  inserting 133
  modifying 139
  outline format 133
  PivotCharts and 149–150
  recommended 129–130
  slicers 137–138
  tabular format 133
placeholders
  for digits 43
  for text, format codes for 44
polynomial trendlines 120
power trendlines 120
Power View Reports, Data Model and 11
PowerPivot
  Data Model and 11
  described 139
  editions available in 139
  hierarchies 145–147
  installing 139, 141
  launching 141
  loading data into 139
  relationships and 142
precedents, tracing 38–39
prerequisite skills and experience for this
  exam 1–2
present value function 90
PRICE function 94
PRICEDISC function 94
PRICEMAT function 94
principal payment (PPMT) function 90
proofing, changing language for 80–81
properties
  for form controls 75
  vs. metadata 24
  workbook connections, viewing 15
protecting workbooks
  current worksheet 22
  described 19
  encryption 27–28
  locking and unlocking 20
  marking as final 28–29
  recommending read-only 29
  sharing and 23
  structure 22

Q

question mark (?), in format codes for numbers 43
quotation marks (" "), in logical tests 88

R

ranges, naming 106
rate of return (RATE) function 90
read-only, recommending 29
RECEIVED function 94
recommended PivotTables 129–130
recommending read-only 29
recording macros 9
recovering versions of workbooks 7
#REF! 35
references, circular 26
refreshing workbook connections 14
regional date and time settings 50
regression analysis 120
rejecting changes 31
relational databases, Data Model and 11
relationships
  activating and deactivating 145
  creating 142–144
  deleting 145
  described 142
  editing 144
removing
  auditing arrows 39
  encryption 28
  metadata 76
  workbook connections 14
  workbook metadata 23
renaming hierarchies 147
repetition initiators, in format codes for
    numbers 44
resolving conflicts in shared workbooks 33
restoring workbooks 7
restricting editing 19, 21
results of scenarios, viewing 112–113
reviewing changes to a shared workbook 31
revision marks. *See* change tracking
rounding, numeric format codes for 43
R-squared value 120

S

saving
  charts as templates 128
  consolidation data 115
  Solver parameters in workbooks 109

workbooks as templates 6
workspaces 22
Scenario Manager 111–112
scenarios
  changing cells 111
  constraints and 109
  defining 111–112
  deleting 113
  described 105
  editing 111, 113
  Goal Seek and 106
  inserting 111
  iterative calculations and 107
  merging 112
  results, viewing 112–113
  Solver and 107–109
  watch window and 110
  what-if analysis tools 106
scientific notation, formatting numbers as 44
scoping, conditional formatting rules and 60
ScreenTips, setting language for 80
scroll bar form control 71, 74
SECOND function 102
secondary axis charts 123–126
seconds, codes for formatting 50
securities analysis functions
  arguments 94
  described 93
  time-based calculations and 101
  types 93
security levels for macros 9
selection, scoping by 60
sequence, custom fill 53
serial date values 100–101
series
  fill options 51
  growth, defined 52
  linear, defined 52
set cell, Goal Seek and 106
shading, applying with conditional
    formatting 58–59
shared workbooks
  accessibility and 76
  change tracking and 17
  comments and 32
  considerations 16
  distributing 76
  editing restrictions 19
  managing changes 30
  merging 33
  protection and 19, 23
  resolving conflicts 33
  reviewing changes 31
  tables and 17

Simplex LP solving method 109
Single Document Interface 22
skills and knowledge assumed for this exam 2
slash (/), in format codes for numbers 44
slicer buttons 4
slicers
   clearing 138
   described 137
   formatting 138
   inserting 138
   macros and 138
   modifying 139
SLN function 92
smoothing trendlines 121
Solver
   described 107
   loading the add-in 110
   methods 109
   saving parameters in workbooks 109
   solving limits 109
sorting data 134–135
sorting PivotCharts 152
spell checking in other languages 81
spin button form control 71, 74
SQL Server, connecting to 12
status, checking for external references 15
Step button, Goal Seek and 106
step values for a series 52
straight-line depreciation 92–93
structure of workbooks, protecting 22
styles
   body, fonts for 83
   cells. *See* cell styles
   copying between workbooks 9
   custom 7
   heading, fonts for 83
   merging 8
   PivotCharts, applying to 152–153
SUMIF function 88
SUMIFS function
   described 89
   syntax 88
sum-of-the-year's-digits depreciation 92–93
SYD function 92
symbols, international 82–83
syntax
   AND function 87
   AVERAGEIF function 88
   AVERAGEIFS function 88
   COUNTIF function 88
   COUNTIFS function 88
   for date format codes 48

   depreciation functions 92
   HLOOKUP function 96
   IF function 87
   investment functions 90
   nested functions 87
   NETWORKDAYS function 104
   for number format codes 45
   OR function 87
   SUMIF function 88
   SUMIFS function 88
   for time format codes 50
   VLOOKUP function 96
   WORKDAY function 104

T

tab order of objects 73
tables
   See also PivotTables
   connecting 142
   data models and 140, 142
   described 119
   relationships between 144
targets, in Solver models 107
tax calculations, depreciation 92
TBILLEQ function 94
TBILLPRICE function 94
TBILLYIELD function 94
templates
   charts 127–128
   color schemes 66
   copying styles between 7
   default storage location 5, 64, 127
   described 4, 63
   modifying 64
   online, creating workbooks from 4
   protecting with passwords 63–64
   saving 63
   saving workbooks as 6
   searching for 4–5
text
   concatenating in formulas 103
   importing as data 11, 13
text placeholders, format codes for 44
themes
   creating 69
   custom 69, 83
   default storage location 68
   described 68
   editing 69–70
   merging styles and 8

Thesaurus 80
thousands separator (,), in format codes for
 numbers 44
time
 elapsed, format codes for 51
 formats, custom 49–51
 functions for calculating. *See* functions
 how Excel calculates 49, 100
 regional settings 50
TIMEVALUE function 102, 105
TODAY function 101, 104
top/bottom rules
 described 55
 modifying default formats 56
tracing
 dependents 38–39
 errors 36–37
 precedents 38–39
tracking changes
 accepting revisions 31
 change history log 17–18
 described 16
 displaying all 31
 exclusions 17
 options 16, 18
 passwords and 17
 rejecting revisions 31
 reviewing 31
 scope 17
 sharing and 17
 tables and 17
 turning off 19
 turning on 18
translating
 options 81
 procedure for 82
TRANSPOSE function
 described 98
 inserting 99
transposing during paste operations 99
trendlines
 adding 120, 122
 chart types available for 120
 deleting 123
 described 120
 effects 121
 forecasting with 121–122
 formatting lines and arrows 121–122
 options 121
 smoothing 121
 types 120
troubleshooting formula errors 37
TRUE, as result of logical operation 87–88

U
underscore (_), in format codes for numbers 44–45
unlocking worksheets 19–20
unsaved workbooks, recovering 7
updating links 12, 15
up-down bars 122

V
#VALUE 35
value fields, scoping by 60
VDB function 92
versions of workbooks
 managing 6
 recovering 7
VLOOKUP function 96–97
volatile functions 101

W
watch window 110
web, importing data from 11, 13
WEEKDAY function 103
weekends, calculating dates and 104
what-if analysis 26, 106
workbooks
 accepting and rejecting changes 31
 accessibility 76–78
 calculating current 27
 calculations 25, 27
 connection properties, viewing 15
 connections, adding 14
 encrypting 27
 Excel Services, making available to 14
 inspecting 23–24, 78
 locking 19
 macros, copying between 9–10
 marking as final 29
 merging 33–35
 metadata, removing 23
 online templates, creating from 4–5
 preparing for review 16, 34
 restricting editing on 19
 reviewing changes 31
 saving as templates 6, 64
 sharing 23
 structure, protecting 22
 styles, copying between 9
 unlocking 19
 versions, retrieving 6

WORKDAY function 103–104
WORKDAY.INTL function 104
worksheets
    calculating current 27
    protecting 22
workspaces, saving 22

X

.xltx file type 63
XML, importing 12

Y

YEAR function 102
YIELD function 94
YIELDDISC function 94
YIELDMAT function 94

Z

zero (0), in format codes for numbers 43

About the author

 Mark Dodge has been working with and writing about Microsoft software since 1989. He is coauthor of *Microsoft Excel 3 Companion*, and is coauthor of the Microsoft Press titles *Microsoft Office Excel 2013 Inside Out* and *Microsoft Office Professional 2013 Step by Step*. As a senior writer at Microsoft, he created print, online, and multimedia documentation for various applications, including Excel and PowerPoint. He is currently on contract researching and writing emergency management plans for FEMA. Mark is a lifelong jazz and rock musician, in addition to an award-winning fine-art photographer.

Now that you've read the book...

Tell us what you think!

Was it useful?
Did it teach you what you wanted to learn?
Was there room for improvement?

Let us know at http://aka.ms/tellpress

Your feedback goes directly to the staff at Microsoft Press,
and we read every one of your responses. Thanks in advance!